Word

For Windows® 95

Simplified™

D1396514

IDG's **3-D Visual**™ Series

IDG BOOKS

From **maranGraphics**™

IDG Books Worldwide, Inc.
An International Data Group Company
Foster City, CA • Indianapolis • Braintree, MA • Chicago • Dallas

Word for Windows® 95 Simplified™

Published by
IDG Books Worldwide, Inc.
An International Data Group Company
919 E. Hillsdale Blvd., Suite 400
Foster City, CA 94404
(415) 655-3000

Copyright© 1995 by maranGraphics Inc.
     5755 Coopers Avenue
     Mississauga, Ontario, Canada
     L4Z 1R9

Screen shots reprinted with permission from Microsoft Corporation.

Library of Congress Catalog Card No.: 95-080940
ISBN: 1-56884-681-9
Printed in the United States of America
10 9 8 7 6 5 4 3 2 1

Distributed in the United States by IDG Books Worldwide, Inc.

Distributed by Computer and Technical Books in Miami, Florida, for South America and the Caribbean; by Longman Singapore in Singapore, Malaysia, Thailand, and Korea; by Toppan Co. Ltd. in Japan; by IDG Communications HK in Hong Kong; by WoodsLane Pty. Ltd. in Australia and New Zealand; and by Transworld Publishers Ltd. in the U.K. and Europe.

For general information on IDG Books in the U.S., including information on discounts and premiums, contact IDG Books at 800-762-2974 or 317-895-5200.

For U.S. Corporate Sales and quantity discounts, contact maranGraphics at 800-469-6616, ext. 206.

For information on international sales of IDG Books, contact Helen Saraceni at 415-655-3021, Fax number 415-655-3295.

For information on translations, contact Marc Jeffrey Mikulich, Director of Rights and Licensing, at IDG Books Worldwide. Fax Number 415-655-3295.

For sales inquiries and special prices for bulk quantities, write to the address above or call IDG Books Worldwide at 415-655-3000.

For information on using IDG Books in the classroom, or ordering examination copies, contact Jim Kelly at 800-434-2086.

Trademark Acknowledgments

The animated characters are the copyright of maranGraphics, Inc.

U.S. Corporate Sales	**U.S. Trade Sales**
Contact maranGraphics at (800) 469-6616, ext. 206 or Fax (905) 890-9434.	Contact IDG Books at (800) 434-3422 or (415) 655-3000.

About IDG Books Worldwide

Welcome to the world of IDG Books Worldwide.

IDG Books Worldwide, Inc., is a subsidiary of International Data Group, the world's largest publisher of business and computer-related information and the leading global provider of information services on information technology. IDG was founded more than 25 years ago and now employs more than 5,700 people worldwide. IDG publishes more than 200 computer publications in 63 countries (see listing below). Forty million people read one or more IDG publications each month.

Launched in 1990, IDG Books is today the fastest-growing publisher of computer and business books in the United States. We are proud to have received 3 awards from the Computer Press Association in recognition of editorial excellence, and our best-selling ...For Dummies series has more than 10 million copies in print with translations in more than 20 languages. IDG Books, through a recent joint venture with IDG's Hi-Tech Beijing, became the first U.S. publisher to publish a computer book in the People's Republic of China. In record time, IDG Books has become the first choice for millions of readers around the world who want to learn how to better manage their businesses.

Our mission is simple: Every IDG book is designed to bring extra value and skill-building instructions to the reader. Our books are written by experts who understand and care about our readers. The knowledge base of our editorial staff comes from years of experience in publishing, education, and journalism — experience which we use to produce books for the '90s. In short, we care about books, so we attract the best people. We devote special attention to details such as audience, interior design, use of icons, and illustrations. And because we use an efficient process of authoring, editing, and desktop publishing our books electronically, we can spend more time ensuring superior content and spend less time on the technicalities of making books.

You can count on our commitment to deliver high-quality books at competitive prices on topics customers want to read about. At IDG, we value quality, and we have been delivering quality for more than 25 years. You'll find no better book on a subject than an IDG book.

John Kilcullen
President and CEO
IDG Books Worldwide, Inc.

IDG Books Worldwide, Inc., is a subsidiary of International Data Group. The officers are Patrick J. McGovern, Founder and Board Chairman; Walter Boyd, President. International Data Group's publications include: ARGENTINA'S Computerworld Argentina, Infoworld Argentina; AUSTRALIA'S Computerworld Australia, Australian PC World, Australian Macworld, Network World, Mobile Business Australia, Reseller, IDG Sources; AUSTRIA'S Computerwelt Oesterreich, PC Test; BRAZIL'S Computerworld, Gamepro, Game Power, Mundo IBM, Mundo Unix, PC World, Super Game; BELGIUM'S Data News (CW) BULGARIA'S Computerworld Bulgaria, Ediworld, PC & Mac World Bulgaria, Network World Bulgaria; CANADA'S CIO Canada, Computerworld Canada, Graduate Computerworld, InfoCanada, Network World Canada; CHILE'S Computerworld Chile, Informatica; COLOMBIA'S Computerworld Colombia, PC World; CZECH REPUBLIC'S Computerworld, Elektronika, PC World; DENMARK'S Communications World, Computerworld Danmark, Macintosh Produktkatalog, Macworld Danmark, PC World Danmark, PC World Produktguide, Tech World, Windows World; ECUADOR'S PC World Ecuador; EGYPT'S Computerworld (CW) Middle East, PC World Middle East; FINLAND'S MikroPC, Tietoviikko, Tietoverkko; FRANCE'S Distributique, GOLDEN MAC, InfoPC, Languages & Systems, Le Guide du Monde Informatique, Le Monde Informatique, Telecoms & Reseaux; GERMANY'S Computerwoche, Computerwoche Focus, Computerwoche Extra, Computerwoche Karriere, Information Management, Macwelt, Netzwelt, PC Welt, PC Woche, Publish, Unit; GREECE'S Infoworld, PC Games; HUNGARY'S Computerworld SZT, PC World; HONG KONG'S Computerworld Hong Kong, PC World Hong Kong; INDIA'S Computers & Communications; IRELAND'S ComputerScope; ISRAEL'S Computerworld Israel, PC World Israel; ITALY'S Computerworld Italia, Lotus Magazine, Macworld Italia, Networking Italia, PC Shopping, PC World Italia; JAPAN'S Computerworld Today, Information Systems World, Macworld Japan, Nikkei Personal Computing, SunWorld Japan, Windows World; KENYA'S East African Computer News; KOREA'S Computerworld Korea, Macworld Korea, PC World Korea; MEXICO'S Compu Edicion, Compu Manufactura, Computacion/Punto de Venta, Computerworld Mexico, MacWorld, Mundo Unix, PC World, Windows; THE NETHERLANDS' Computer! Totaal, Computable (CW), LAN Magazine, MacWorld, Totaal "Windows"; NEW ZEALAND'S Computer Listings, Computerworld New Zealand, New Zealand PC World, Network World; NIGERIA'S PC World Africa; NORWAY'S Computerworld Norge, C/World, Lotusworld Norge, Macworld Norge, Networld, PC World Ekspress, PC World Norge, PC World's Produktguide, Publish& Multimedia World, Student Data, Unix World, Windowsworld; IDG Direct Response; PAKISTAN'S PC World Pakistan; PANAMA'S PC World Panama; PERU'S Computerworld Peru, PC World; PEOPLE'S REPUBLIC OF CHINA'S China Computerworld, China Infoworld, Electronics Today/Multimedia World, Electronics International, Electronic Product World, China Network World, PC and Communications Magazine, PC World China, Software World Magazine, Telecom Product World; IDG HIGH TECH BEIJING'S New Product World; PHILIPPINES' Computerworld Philippines, PC Digest (PCW); POLAND'S Computerworld Poland, PC World/Komputer; PORTUGAL'S Cerebro/PC World, Correio Informatico/Computerworld, Informatica & Comunicacoes Catalogo, MacIn, Nacional de Produtos; ROMANIA'S Computerworld, PC World; RUSSIA'S Computerworld-Moscow, Mir - PC, Sety; SINGAPORE'S Computerworld Southeast Asia, PC World Singapore; SLOVENIA'S Monitor Magazine; SOUTH AFRICA'S Computer Mail (CIO),Computing S.A.,Network World S.A., Software World; SPAIN'S Advanced Systems, Amiga World, Computerworld Espana, Communicaciones World, Macworld Espana, NeXTWORLD, Super Juegos Magazine (GamePro), PC World Espana, Publish; SWEDEN'S Attack, ComputerSweden, Corporate Computing, Natverk & Kommunikation, Macworld, Mikrodatorn, PC World, Publishing & Design (CAP), Datalngenjoren, Maxi Data,Windows World; SWITZERLAND'S Computerworld Schweiz, Macworld Schweiz, PC Tip; TAIWAN'S Computerworld Taiwan, PC World Taiwan; THAILAND'S Thai Computerworld; TURKEY'S Computerworld Monitor, Macworld Turkiye, PC World Turkiye; UKRAINE'S Computerworld; UNITED KINGDOM'S Computing /Computerworld, Connexion/Network World, Lotus Magazine, Macworld, Open Computing/Sunworld; UNITED STATES' Advanced Systems, AmigaWorld, Cable in the Classroom, CD Review, CIO, Computerworld, Digital Video, DOS Resource Guide, Electronic Entertainment Magazine, Federal Computer Week, Federal Integrator, GamePro, IDG Books, Infoworld, Infoworld Direct, Laser Event, Macworld, Multimedia World, Network World, PC Letter, PC World, PlayRight, Power PC World, Publish, SWATPro, Video Event; VENEZUELA'S Computerworld Venezuela, PC World; VIETNAM'S PC World Vietnam

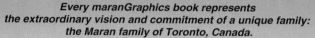

Every maranGraphics book represents the extraordinary vision and commitment of a unique family: the Maran family of Toronto, Canada.

Back Row (from left to right): Sherry Maran, Rob Maran, mG, Richard Maran, Maxine Maran, Jill Maran.

Front Row (from left to right): mG, Judy Maran, Ruth Maran, mG.

Richard Maran is the company founder and its inspirational leader. He developed maranGraphics' proprietary communication technology called "visual grammar." This book is built on that technology—empowering readers with the easiest and quickest way to learn about computers.

Ruth Maran is the Author and Architect—a role Richard established that now bears Ruth's distinctive touch. She creates the words and visual structure that are the basis for the books.

Judy Maran is Senior Editor. She works with Ruth, Richard, and the highly talented maranGraphics illustrators, designers, and editors to transform Ruth's material into its final form.

Rob Maran is the Technical and Production Specialist. He makes sure the state-of-the-art technology used to create these books always performs as it should.

Sherry Maran manages the Reception, Order Desk, and any number of areas that require immediate attention and a helping hand.

Jill Maran is a jack-of-all-trades and dynamo who fills in anywhere she's needed anytime she's back from university.

Maxine Maran is the Business Manager and family sage. She maintains order in the business and family—and keeps everything running smoothly.

Oh, and there's **mG**. He's maranGraphics' spokesperson and, well, star. When you use a maranGraphics book, you'll see a lot of mG and his friends. They're just part of the family!

Credits

Author:
Ruth Maran

Copy Developer:
Kelleigh Wing

Technical Consultant:
Wendi Blouin Ewbank

Editors:
Brad Hilderley
Paul Lofthouse

Layout Designer:
Christie Van Duin

Illustrators:
Tamara Poliquin
Chris K.C. Leung
Russell Marini
Andrew Trowbridge
Dave Ross
David de Haas

Indexer:
Mark Kmetzko

Post Production:
Robert Maran

Acknowledgments

Thanks to the dedicated staff of maranGraphics, including
Brad Hilderley, Chris K.C. Leung, Paul Lofthouse, Jill Maran,
Judy Maran, Maxine Maran, Robert Maran, Sherry Maran,
Russ Marini, Tamara Poliquin, Andrew Trowbridge,
Christie Van Duin, and Kelleigh Wing.

Finally, to Richard Maran who originated the easy-to-use graphic
format of this guide. Thank you for your inspiration and guidance.

TABLE OF CONTENTS

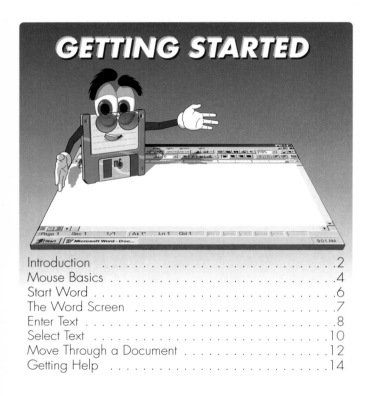

GETTING STARTED

SAVE AND OPEN YOUR DOCUMENTS

EDIT YOUR DOCUMENTS

SMART EDITING

CHANGE YOUR DOCUMENT DISPLAY

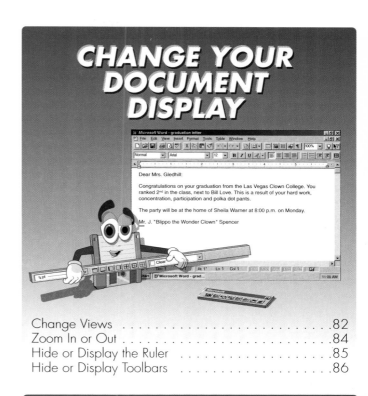

PRINT YOUR DOCUMENTS

USING MULTIPLE DOCUMENTS

TABLE OF CONTENTS

FORMAT CHARACTERS

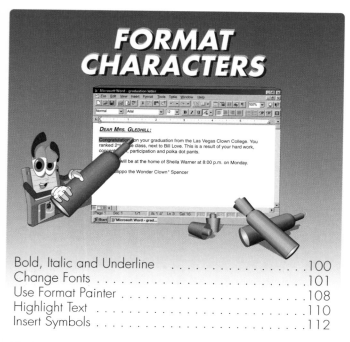

FORMAT PARAGRAPHS

FORMAT PAGES

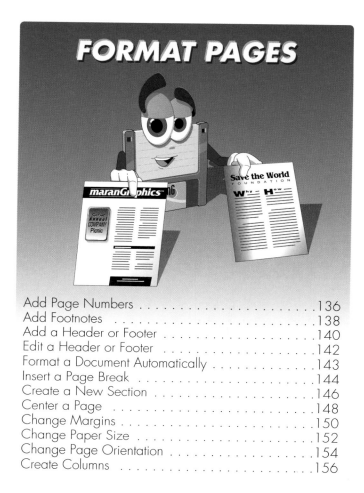

WORKING WITH TABLES

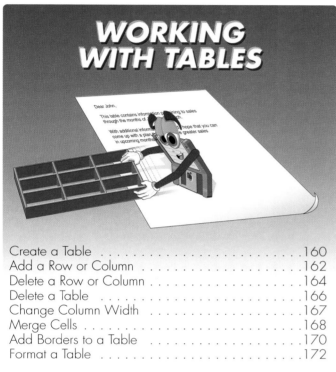

MERGE DOCUMENTS

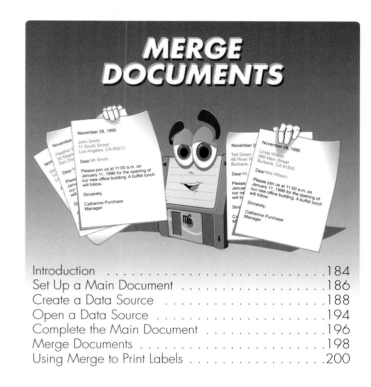

TIME SAVING FEATURES

Word for Windows® 95 offers many features to help you create professional-looking documents quickly and efficiently.

You can use Word to create letters, reports, manuals, newsletters and brochures.

EDITING

Word offers many features to help you produce documents more efficiently, such as automatic spell checking and correction.

Note: For more information, refer to the editing chapters, starting on page 36.

FORMATTING

Word offers many features to help you change the appearance of text in your documents.

Note: For more information, refer to the formatting chapters, starting on page 100.

TABLES

You can create tables to organize information.

Note: For more information, refer to the Working with Tables chapter, starting on page 160.

MAIL MERGE

You can quickly produce personalized letters and mailing labels for each person on a mailing list.

Note: For more information, refer to the Merge Documents chapter, starting on page 184.

3

The mouse is a hand-held device that lets you select and move items on your screen.

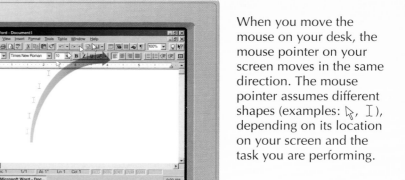

When you move the mouse on your desk, the mouse pointer on your screen moves in the same direction. The mouse pointer assumes different shapes (examples: ⌖, I), depending on its location on your screen and the task you are performing.

Hold the mouse as shown in the diagram. Use your thumb and two rightmost fingers to move the mouse while your two remaining fingers press the mouse buttons.

REMEMBER THESE MOUSE TERMS

CLICK
Press and release the left mouse button.

DOUBLE-CLICK
Quickly press and release the left mouse button twice.

DRAG AND DROP
When the mouse pointer is over an object on your screen, press and hold down the left mouse button. Still holding down the button, move the mouse to where you want to place the object and then release the button.

Tip

A ball under the mouse senses movement. To ensure smooth motion of the mouse, you should occasionally remove and clean this ball.

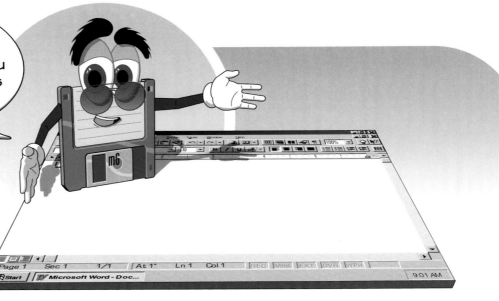

When you start Word, a blank document appears. You can type text into this document.

START WORD

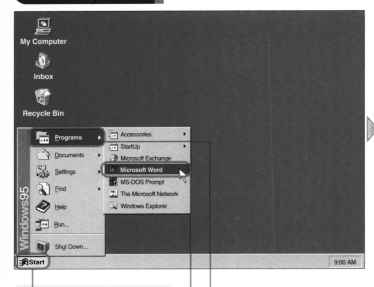

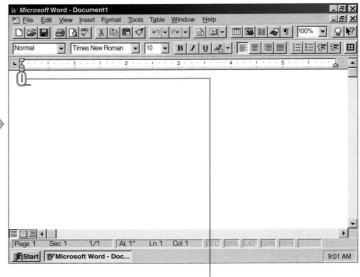

1 Move the mouse over **Start** and then press the left button.

2 Move the mouse over **Programs**.

3 Move the mouse over **Microsoft Word** and then press the left button.

◆ The **Microsoft Word** window appears, displaying a blank document.

◆ The flashing line on your screen indicates where the text you type will appear. It is called the **insertion point**.

6

When you start Word, the screen displays several items to help you perform tasks efficiently.

THE WORD SCREEN

STANDARD TOOLBAR

Contains buttons to help you quickly select commonly used commands, such as opening a document.

FORMATTING TOOLBAR

Contains buttons to help you quickly select formatting and layout features, such as **bold** and <u>underline</u>.

RULER

Allows you to change margin and tab settings for your document.

STATUS BAR

Displays information about the area of the document displayed on your screen and the position of the insertion point.

Page 1
The page displayed on your screen.

Sec 1
The section of the document displayed on your screen.

1/1
The page displayed on the screen and the total number of pages in the document.

At 1"
The distance (in inches) from the top of the page to the insertion point.

Ln 1
The number of lines from the top of the page to the insertion point.

Col 1
The number of characters from the left margin to the insertion point, including spaces.

Word lets you type text into your document quickly and easily.

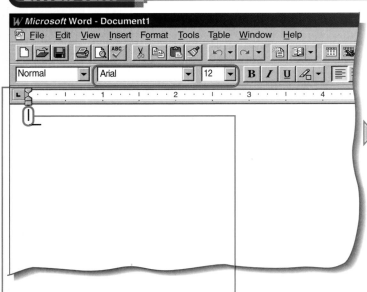

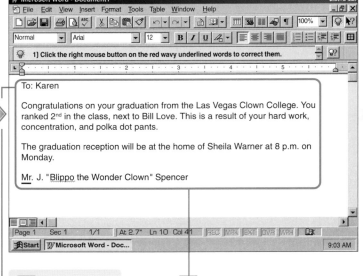

To: Karen

Congratulations on your graduation from the Las Vegas Clown College. You ranked 2nd in the class, next to Bill Love. This is a result of your hard work, concentration, and polka dot pants.

The graduation reception will be at the home of Sheila Warner at 8 p.m. on Monday.

Mr. J. "Blippo the Wonder Clown" Spencer

◆ In this book, the design and size of text were changed to make the document easier to read. To change the design and size of text, refer to page 104.

◆ The flashing line on your screen is called the **insertion point**. It indicates where the text you type will appear.

1 Type the first line of text.

2 To start a new paragraph, press **Enter** on your keyboard twice.

3 Type the remaining text.

◆ When you reach the end of a line, Word automatically wraps the text to the next line. You only need to press **Enter** when you want to start a new line or paragraph.

8

- Introduction
- Mouse Basics
- Start Word
- The Word Screen

- **Enter Text**
- Select Text
- Move Through a Document
- Getting Help

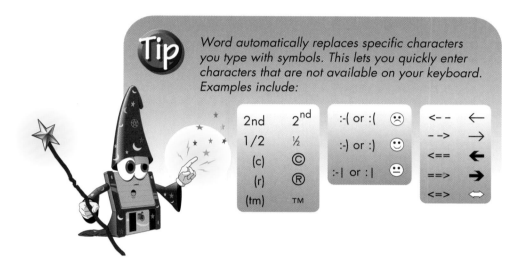

Tip

Word automatically replaces specific characters you type with symbols. This lets you quickly enter characters that are not available on your keyboard. Examples include:

2nd	2nd
1/2	½
(c)	©
(r)	®
(tm)	™

:-(or :(	☹
:-) or :)	☺
:-| or :|	😐

<- -	←
- ->	→
<==	⬅
==>	➡
<=>	⬌

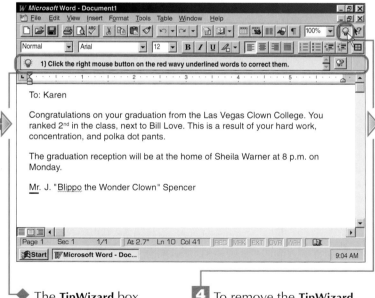

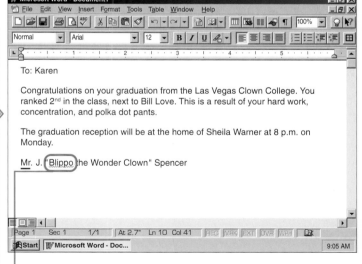

◆ The **TipWizard** box displays information and tips about the tasks you are performing.

4 To remove the **TipWizard** box from your screen, move the mouse ⇧ over 💡 and then press the left button.

Note: Removing the TipWizard box from your screen provides a larger and less cluttered working area.

◆ If text in your document appears with a red underline, Word does not recognize the word and considers it misspelled.

Note: For information on misspelled words, refer to page 54.

9

SELECT TEXT

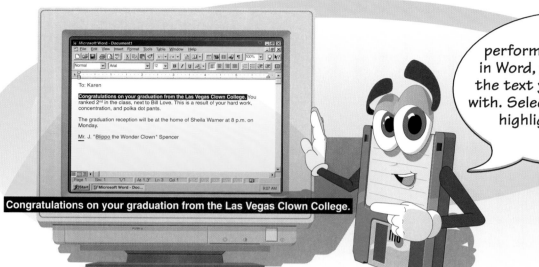

Before performing many tasks in Word, you must select the text you want to work with. Selected text appears highlighted on your screen.

Congratulations on your graduation from the Las Vegas Clown College.

SELECT TEXT

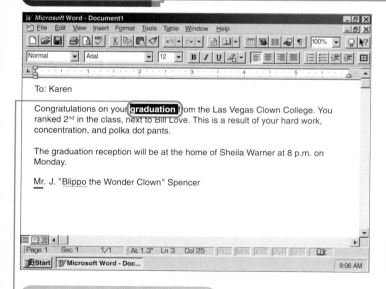

SELECT A WORD

1 Move the mouse I anywhere over the word you want to select and then quickly press the left button twice.

◆ To cancel a text selection, move the mouse I outside the selected area and then press the left button.

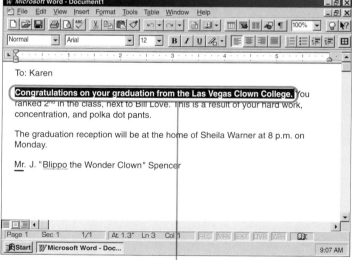

SELECT A SENTENCE

1 Press and hold down Ctrl on your keyboard.

2 Still holding down Ctrl, move the mouse I anywhere over the sentence you want to select and then press the left button. Then release Ctrl.

- Introduction
- Mouse Basics
- Start Word
- The Word Screen
- Enter Text
- **Select Text**
- Move Through a Document
- Getting Help

Tip

To quickly select all the text in your document, press and hold down `Ctrl` and then press `A` on your keyboard. Then release the keys.

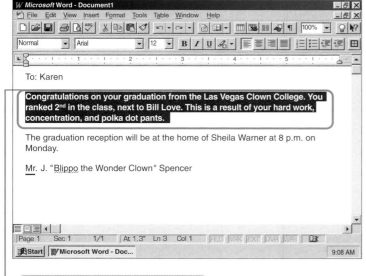

SELECT A PARAGRAPH

1 Move the mouse I anywhere over the paragraph you want to select and then quickly press the left button **three** times.

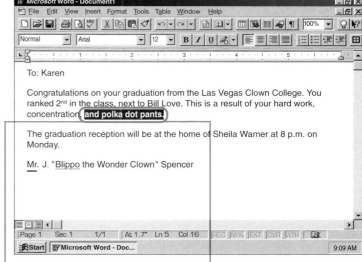

SELECT ANY AMOUNT OF TEXT

1 Move the mouse I over the first word you want to select.

2 Press and hold down the left button as you drag the mouse I over the text you want to select. Then release the button.

MOVE THROUGH A DOCUMENT

> If you create a long document, your computer screen cannot display all the text at the same time. You must scroll up or down to view and edit other parts of the document.

MOVE THE INSERTION POINT

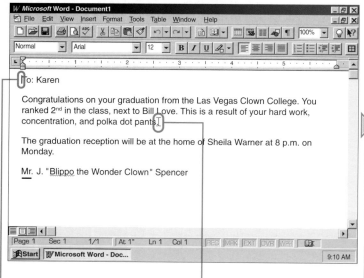

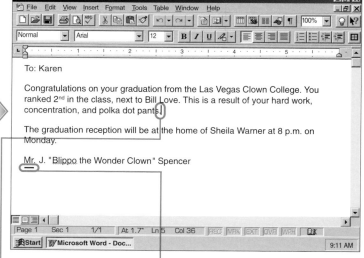

◆ The insertion point indicates where the text you type will appear in the document.

1 Move the mouse I to where you want to place the insertion point and then press the left button.

◆ The insertion point appears in the new position.

Note: You can also press ↓, ↑, ← or → on your keyboard to move one line or character in any direction.

◆ You cannot move the insertion point below the horizontal line displayed on your screen. To move this line, position the insertion point after the last character in your document and then press **Enter** several times.

- Introduction
- Mouse Basics
- Start Word
- The Word Screen
- Enter Text
- Select Text
- **Move Through a Document**
- Getting Help

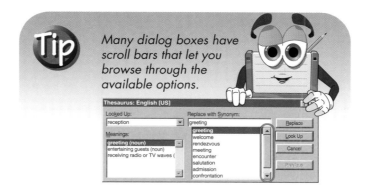

Many dialog boxes have scroll bars that let you browse through the available options.

SCROLL UP OR DOWN

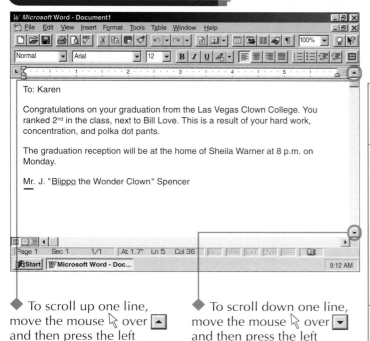

◆ To scroll up one line, move the mouse over ▲ and then press the left button.

◆ To scroll down one line, move the mouse over ▼ and then press the left button.

SCROLL TO ANY POSITION

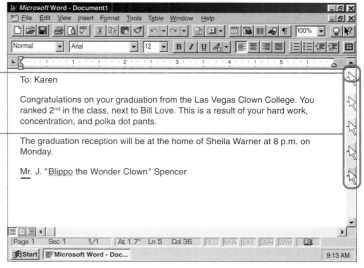

1 To quickly scroll through your document, move the mouse over the scroll box (▢).

2 Press and hold down the left button and then move the mouse down the scroll bar. Then release the button.

Note: The location of the scroll box indicates which part of the document you are viewing. For example, to view the middle of the document, drag the scroll box half way down the scroll bar.

GETTING HELP

> If you do not know how to perform a task, you can use the Help feature to get information.

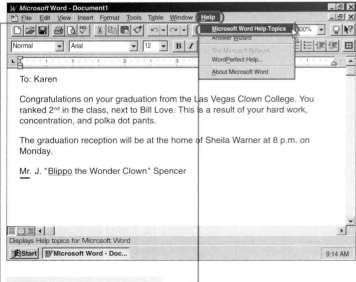

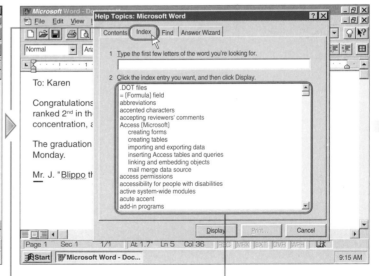

1 Move the mouse ⌖ over **Help** and then press the left button.

2 Move the mouse ⌖ over **Microsoft Word Help Topics** and then press the left button.

◆ The **Help Topics** dialog box appears.

3 To display the help index, move the mouse ⌖ over the **Index** tab and then press the left button.

◆ This area displays a list of all the available help topics.

14

- Introduction
- Mouse Basics
- Start Word
- The Word Screen
- Enter Text
- Select Text
- Move Through a Document
- **Getting Help**

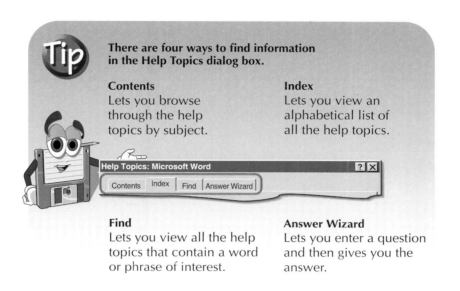

There are four ways to find information in the Help Topics dialog box.

Contents
Lets you browse through the help topics by subject.

Index
Lets you view an alphabetical list of all the help topics.

Find
Lets you view all the help topics that contain a word or phrase of interest.

Answer Wizard
Lets you enter a question and then gives you the answer.

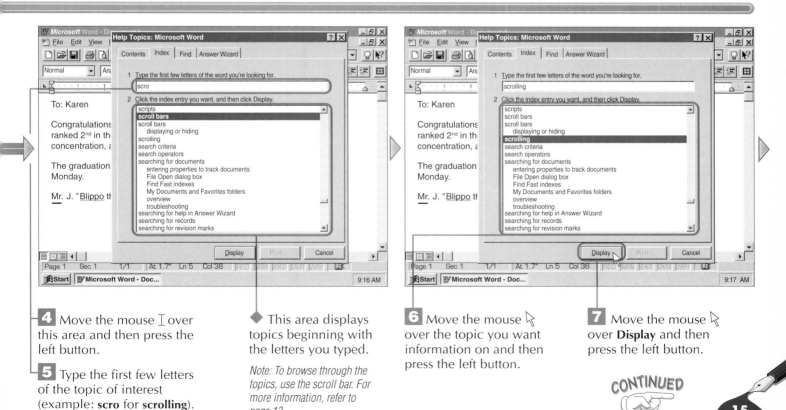

4 Move the mouse I over this area and then press the left button.

5 Type the first few letters of the topic of interest (example: **scro** for **scrolling**).

◆ This area displays topics beginning with the letters you typed.

Note: To browse through the topics, use the scroll bar. For more information, refer to page 13.

6 Move the mouse ⤷ over the topic you want information on and then press the left button.

7 Move the mouse ⤷ over **Display** and then press the left button.

CONTINUED

The Help feature saves you time by eliminating the need to refer to other sources.

GETTING HELP (CONTINUED)

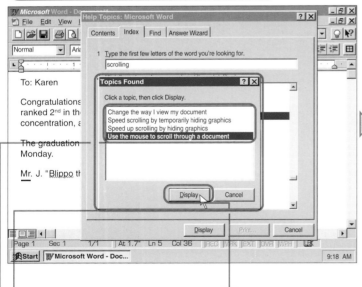

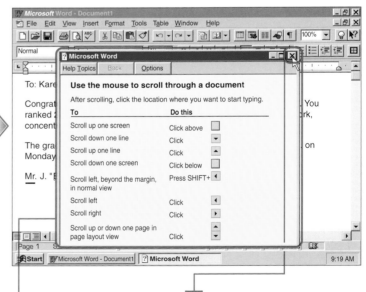

◆ This window displays items related to the topic you selected.

8 Move the mouse ⟨ over the item you want information on and then press the left button.

9 Move the mouse ⟨ over **Display** and then press the left button.

◆ This window displays information on the item you selected.

10 To close the window, move the mouse ⟨ over ☒ and then press the left button.

- Introduction
- Mouse Basics
- Start Word
- The Word Screen
- Enter Text
- Select Text
- Move Through a Document
- **Getting Help**

You can display a description of a button on your screen.

GETTING HELP ON A BUTTON

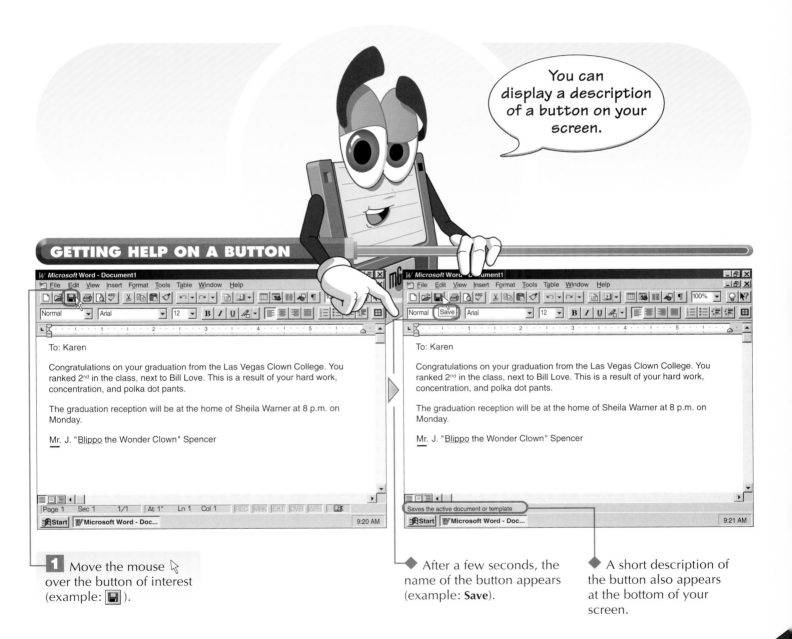

1 Move the mouse over the button of interest (example: 📋).

◆ After a few seconds, the name of the button appears (example: **Save**).

◆ A short description of the button also appears at the bottom of your screen.

17

SAVE AND OPEN YOUR DOCUMENTS

HARD DRIVE (C:)

The hard drive is the primary device your computer uses to store information.

Most computers come with one hard drive, located inside the computer case. The hard drive is usually called drive C.

Like a filing cabinet, your hard drive uses folders to organize information. A folder usually stores related information and can contain documents and other folders.

FLOPPY DRIVE (A:)

A floppy drive stores and retrieves information on floppy disks (diskettes). If your computer has only one floppy drive, the drive is called drive A. If your computer has two floppy drives, the second drive is called drive B.

CD-ROM DRIVE (D:)

A CD-ROM drive is a device that reads information stored on compact discs. You cannot change information stored on a compact disc.

Note: Your computer may not have a CD-ROM drive.

You should save your document to store it for future use. This lets you later retrieve the document for reviewing or editing.

SAVE A DOCUMENT

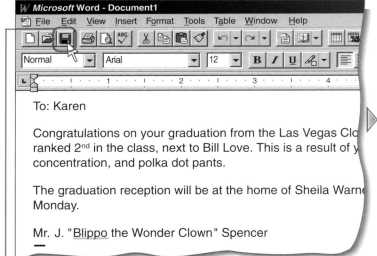

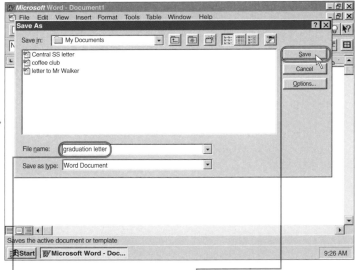

1 Move the mouse ⤵ over 🖫 and then press the left button.

◆ The **Save As** dialog box appears.

*Note: If you previously saved your document, the **Save As** dialog box will not appear, since you have already named the document.*

2 Type a name for your document.

*Note: You can use up to 255 characters to name a document. The name cannot contain the characters / \ > < * ? " ; : or |.*

3 Move the mouse ⤵ over **Save** and then press the left button.

To avoid losing your work, you should save your document approximately every 10 minutes.

SAVE YOUR CHANGES

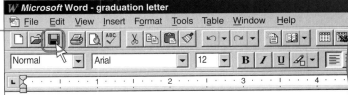

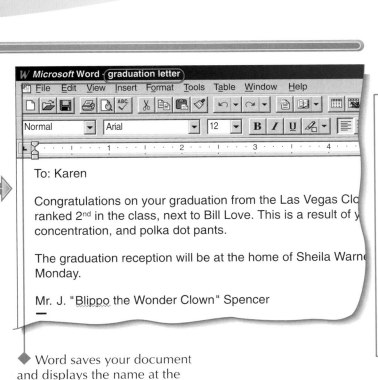

To: Karen

Congratulations on your graduation from the Las Vegas Clo ranked 2nd in the class, next to Bill Love. This is a result of y concentration, and polka dot pants.

The graduation reception will be at the home of Sheila Warne Monday.

Mr. J. "Blippo the Wonder Clown" Spencer

◆ Word saves your document and displays the name at the top of your screen.

To: Karen

Congratulations on your graduation from the Las Vegas Clo ranked 2nd in the class, next to Bill Love. This is a result of y concentration, and polka dot pants.

The graduation reception will be at the home of Sheila Warne Monday.

Mr. J. "Blippo the Wonder Clown" Spencer

1 To save your changes, move the mouse over and then press the left button.

SAVE A DOCUMENT TO A FLOPPY DISK

You can save a document to a floppy disk. This is useful if you want to give a copy of a document to a colleague.

SAVE A DOCUMENT TO A FLOPPY DISK

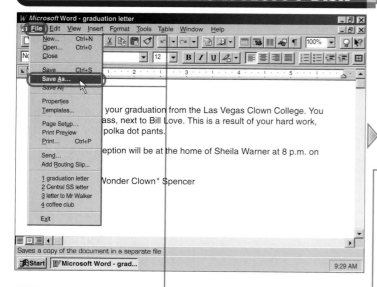

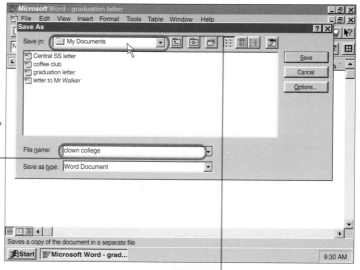

1 Insert a floppy disk into a drive.

2 Move the mouse ⬚ over **File** and then press the left button.

3 Move the mouse ⬚ over **Save As** and then press the left button.

◆ The **Save As** dialog box appears.

4 This area displays the current filename. To save your document with a different name, type a new name.

◆ This area displays the location where the document will be saved.

5 To change the location, move the mouse ⬚ over this area and then press the left button.

- Introduction
- Save a Document
- Save Your Changes
- Save a Document to a Floppy Disk
- Exit Word
- Open a Document
- Find a Document

SAVE A DOCUMENT WITH A NEW NAME

If you plan to make major changes to a document, you may want to save the document with a different name before you begin. This gives you two copies of the document–the original document and a document with all the changes.

1 Perform steps **2** to **4** on page 24.

2 Move the mouse over **Save** and then press the left button.

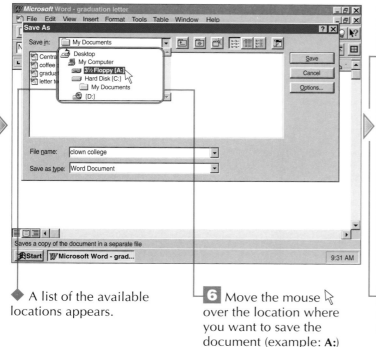

◆ A list of the available locations appears.

6 Move the mouse over the location where you want to save the document (example: **A:**) and then press the left button.

7 To save the document, move the mouse over **Save** and then press the left button.

25

When you finish using Word, you can exit the program.

EXIT WORD

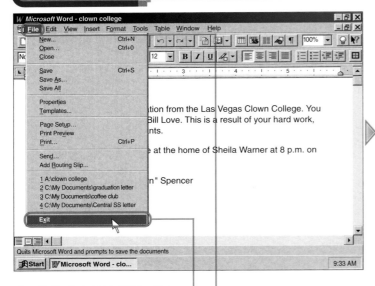

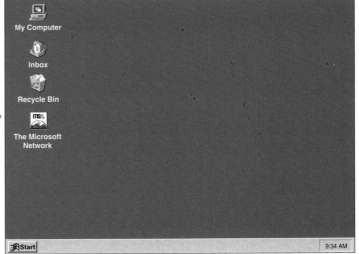

1 Save your document before exiting.

Note: For information on saving, refer to page 22.

2 Move the mouse over **File** and then press the left button.

3 Move the mouse over **Exit** and then press the left button.

◆ The Word window disappears from your screen.

Note: To restart Word, refer to page 6.

◆ To avoid damaging your information, you must always exit Word and Windows before turning off your computer.

- Introduction
- Save a Document
- Save Your Changes
- Save a Document to a Floppy Disk
- **Exit Word**
- **Open a Document**
- Find a Document

Word remembers the names of the last four documents you worked with. You can quickly open any of these documents.

QUICKLY OPEN A DOCUMENT

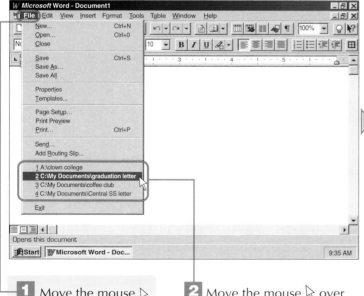

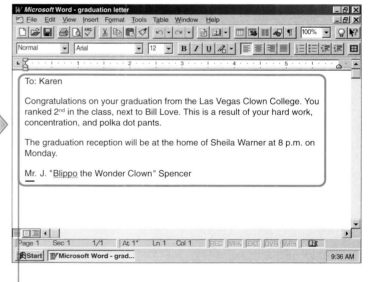

1 Move the mouse ⟋ over **File** and then press the left button.

2 Move the mouse ⟋ over the name of the document you want to open and then press the left button.

◆ Word opens the document and displays it on your screen. You can now review and make changes to the document.

27

You can open a saved document and display it on your screen. This lets you review and make changes to the document.

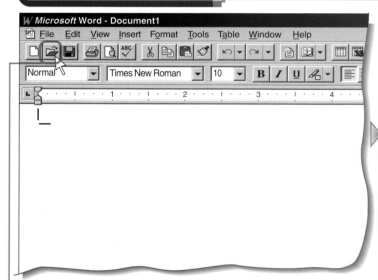

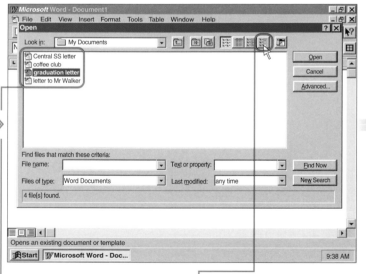

1 Move the mouse ⬚ over 📂 and then press the left button.

◆ The **Open** dialog box appears.

2 Move the mouse ⬚ over the name of the document you want to open and then press the left button.

Note: If the name of the document you want to open is not displayed, refer to page 30 to find the document.

3 To preview the contents of the document, move the mouse ⬚ over 📄 and then press the left button.

28

- Introduction
- Save a Document
- Save Your Changes
- Save a Document to a Floppy Disk
- Exit Word
- Open a Document
- Find a Document

Tip

You can easily open a brand new document at any time.

Note: For more information, refer to page 90.

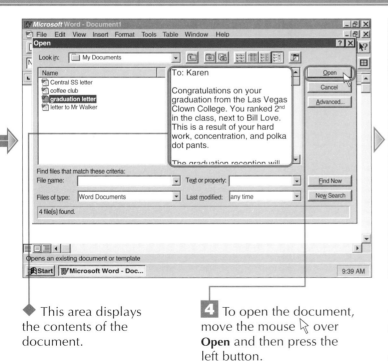

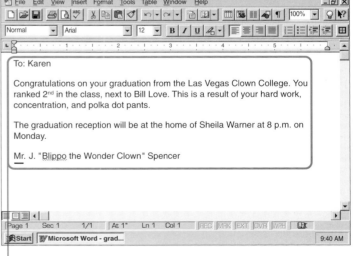

◆ This area displays the contents of the document.

4 To open the document, move the mouse ▷ over **Open** and then press the left button.

◆ Word opens the document and displays it on your screen. You can now review and make changes to the document.

FIND A
DOCUMENT

If you cannot remember the name or location of a document you want to open, you can have Word search for the document.

FIND A DOCUMENT

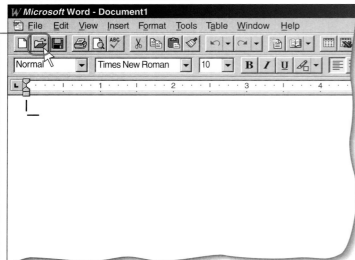

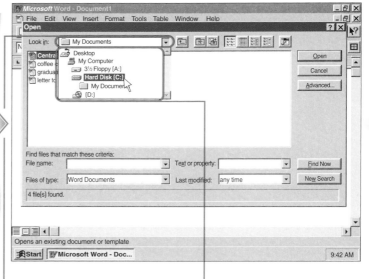

1 Move the mouse ⍈ over 📂 and then press the left button.

◆ The **Open** dialog box appears.

2 To specify where you want Word to search for the document, move the mouse ⍈ over this area and then press the left button.

3 Move the mouse ⍈ over the location you want to search and then press the left button.

SAVE AND OPEN YOUR DOCUMENTS

- Introduction
- Save a Document
- Save Your Changes
- Save a Document to a Floppy Disk

- Exit Word
- Open a Document
- **Find a Document**

Tip

If you search for a document with a particular name, Word will find all the documents with names containing the text you specified.

Find: letter

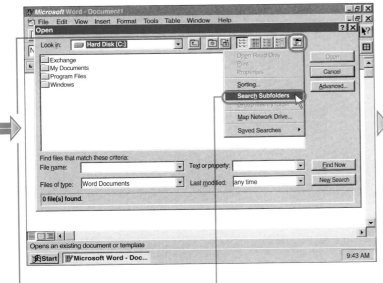

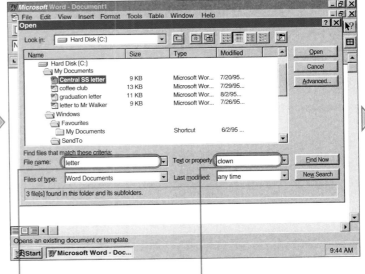

4 To search the contents of all the folders in the location you selected, move the mouse ⬚ over 🔲 and then press the left button.

5 Move the mouse ⬚ over **Search Subfolders** and then press the left button.

*Note: If the area beside **Search Subfolders** displays a check mark (✔), the feature is on. To leave the feature on, press* `Alt` *on your keyboard.*

6 If you know all or part of the name of the document you want to find, move the mouse I over this area and then press the left button. Then type the name (example: **letter**).

7 If you know a word or phrase in the document you want to find, move the mouse I over this area and then press the left button. Then type the word or phrase (example: **clown**).

CONTINUED

31

When the search is complete, Word displays the names of the documents it found.

FIND A DOCUMENT (CONTINUED)

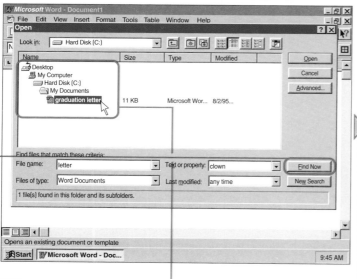

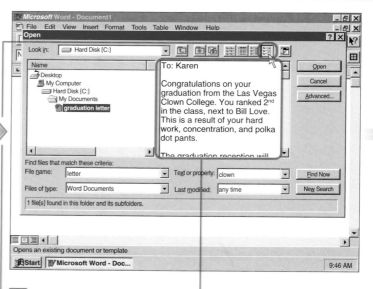

8 To complete the search, move the mouse ⬐ over **Find Now** and then press the left button.

◆ This area displays the names of the documents Word found.

9 Move the mouse ⬐ over the name of a document you want to preview and then press the left button.

10 To preview the contents of the document, move the mouse ⬐ over ▦ and then press the left button.

◆ This area displays the contents of the document.

*Note: To preview the contents of another document, repeat step **9**.*

- Introduction
- Save a Document
- Save Your Changes
- Save a Document to a Floppy Disk
- Exit Word
- Open a Document
- **Find a Document**

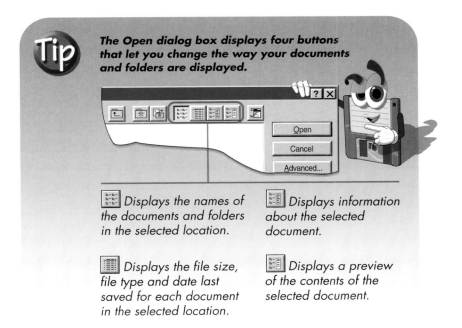

Tip

The Open dialog box displays four buttons that let you change the way your documents and folders are displayed.

Displays the names of the documents and folders in the selected location.

Displays the file size, file type and date last saved for each document in the selected location.

Displays information about the selected document.

Displays a preview of the contents of the selected document.

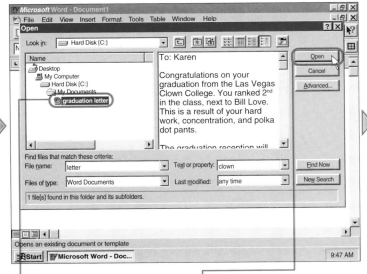

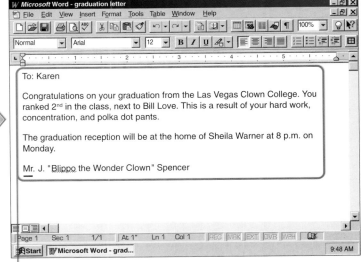

11 To open a document, move the mouse ⩗ over the name of the document and then press the left button.

12 Move the mouse ⩗ over **Open** and then press the left button.

◆ Word opens the document and displays it on your screen. You can now review and make changes to the document.

In this chapter you will learn how to make changes to text in your documents.

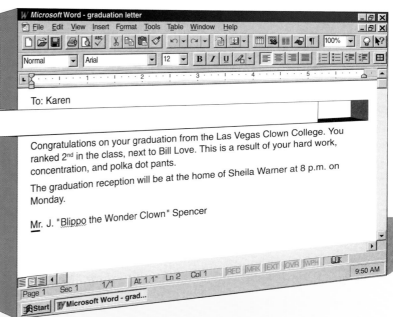

To: Karen

Congratulations on your graduation from the Las Vegas Clown College. You ranked 2nd in the class, next to Bill Love. This is a result of your hard work, concentration, and polka dot pants.

The graduation reception will be at the home of Sheila Warner at 8 p.m. on Monday.

Mr. J. "Blippo the Wonder Clown" Spencer

EDIT YOUR DOCUMENTS

Insert Text

Delete Text

Undo Last Change

Move Text

Copy Text

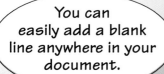

INSERT TEXT

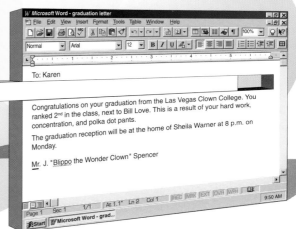

You can easily add a blank line anywhere in your document.

INSERT A BLANK LINE

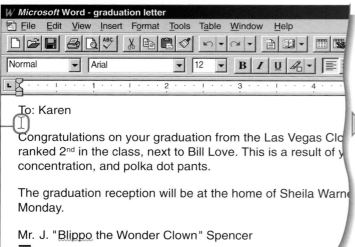

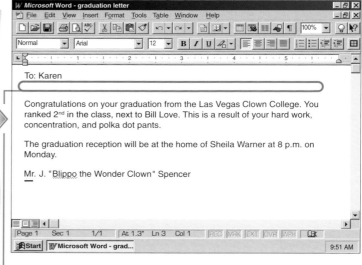

1 Move the mouse I to where you want to insert a blank line and then press the left button.

2 Press **Enter** on your keyboard to insert the blank line.

Note: The text following the blank line moves down one line.

36

- **Insert Text**
- Delete Text
- Undo Last Change
- Move Text
- Copy Text

You can easily split a paragraph in two in order to separate your ideas.

SPLIT A PARAGRAPH

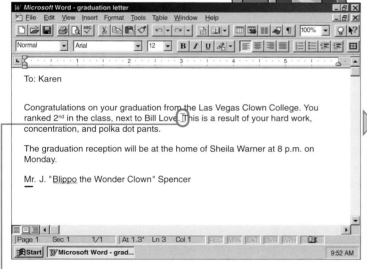

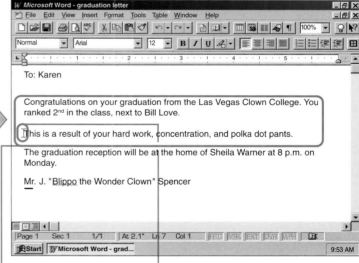

1 Move the mouse I to where you want to split a paragraph in two and then press the left button.

2 Press **Enter** on your keyboard and the paragraph splits in two.

3 To insert a blank line between the paragraphs, press **Enter** again.

JOIN TWO PARAGRAPHS

1 Move the mouse I to the left of the first character in the second paragraph and then press the left button.

2 Press **◆Backspace** on your keyboard until the paragraphs are joined.

37

INSERT TEXT

You can easily add new text to your document. In the Insert mode, the existing text moves to make room for the text you type.

│This sentence moves forward as you type.

---------------------------│This sentence moves forward as you type.

INSERT TEXT

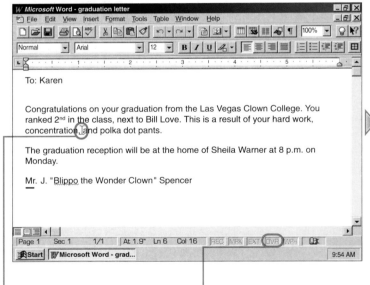

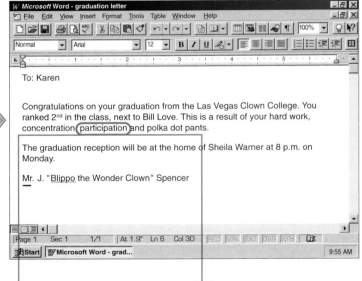

When you start Word, the program is in the Insert mode.

1 Move the mouse I to where you want to insert the new text and then press the left button.

◆ If this area displays **OVR** in black (OVR), press Insert on your keyboard to switch to the Insert mode.

2 Type the text you want to insert (example: **participation**).

3 To insert a blank space, press the **Spacebar**.

Note: The words to the right of the new text move forward.

38

- **Insert Text**
- Delete Text
- Undo Last Change
- Move Text
- Copy Text

In the Overtype mode, you can type over existing text in your document.

|This sentence disappears as you type.

xxxxxxxxxxxxxxxxxxxx|pears as you type.

TYPE OVER TEXT

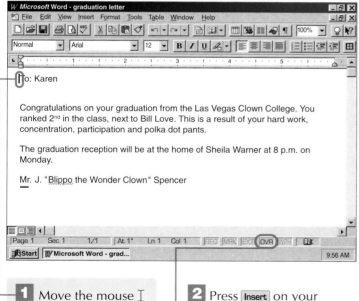

1 Move the mouse I to the left of the first character you want to type over and then press the left button.

2 Press Insert on your keyboard to turn on the Overtype mode.

◆ This area displays **OVR** in black (OVR) when the Overtype mode is on.

3 Type the text you want to replace the existing text.

4 Press Insert on your keyboard to turn off the Overtype mode.

DELETE TEXT

You can easily remove text you no longer need. The remaining text moves to fill any empty spaces.

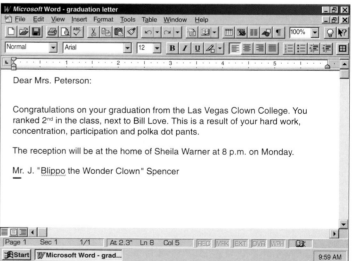

DELETE CHARACTERS

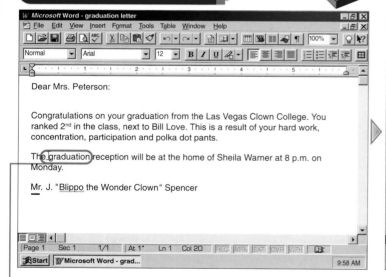

Dear Mrs. Peterson:

Congratulations on your graduation from the Las Vegas Clown College. You ranked 2nd in the class, next to Bill Love. This is a result of your hard work, concentration, participation and polka dot pants.

The graduation reception will be at the home of Sheila Warner at 8 p.m. on Monday.

Mr. J. "Blippo the Wonder Clown" Spencer

Dear Mrs. Peterson:

Congratulations on your graduation from the Las Vegas Clown College. You ranked 2nd in the class, next to Bill Love. This is a result of your hard work, concentration, participation and polka dot pants.

The reception will be at the home of Sheila Warner at 8 p.m. on Monday.

Mr. J. "Blippo the Wonder Clown" Spencer

1 Move the mouse I to the left of the first character you want to delete (example: **g** in graduation) and then press the left button.

2 Press **Delete** on your keyboard once for each character or space you want to delete.

You can also use **←Backspace** to delete characters. Move the mouse I to the **right** of the first character you want to delete and then press the left button. Then press **←Backspace** on your keyboard once for each character or space you want to delete.

40

- Insert Text
- **Delete Text**
- Undo Last Change
- Move Text
- Copy Text

You can remove a blank line from your document. The remaining text moves up one line.

DELETE A BLANK LINE

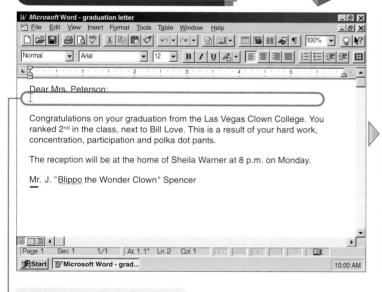

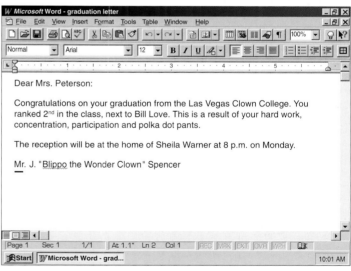

1 Move the mouse I to the beginning of the blank line you want to delete and then press the left button.

2 Press **Delete** on your keyboard to remove the blank line.

Note: The text following the blank line moves up one line.

You can quickly delete a section of text you have selected.

DELETE SELECTED TEXT

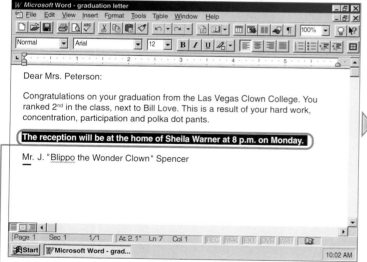

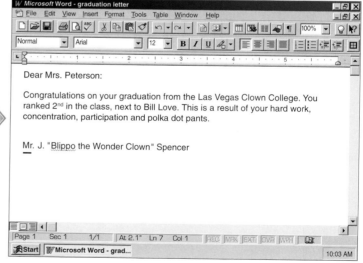

1 Select the text you want to delete.

Note: To select text, refer to page 10.

2 Press **Delete** on your keyboard to remove the text.

42

- Insert Text
- **Delete Text**
- **Undo Last Change**
- Move Text
- Copy Text

> Word remembers the last changes you made to your document. If you regret these changes, you can cancel them by using the Undo feature.

UNDO LAST CHANGE

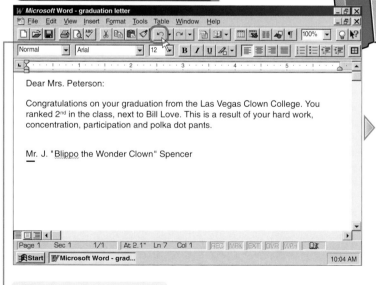

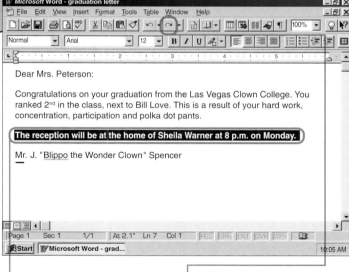

1 Move the mouse over and then press the left button.

Note: The Undo feature can cancel your last editing and formatting changes.

◆ Word cancels the last change you made to your document.

◆ You can repeat step **1** to cancel previous changes you made.

◆ To reverse the results of using the Undo feature, move the mouse over and then press the left button.

43

You can reorganize your document by moving text from one location to another.

MOVE TEXT

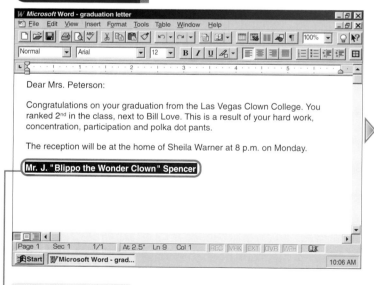

1 Select the text you want to move.

Note: To select text, refer to page 10.

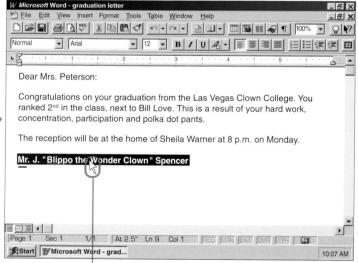

2 Move the mouse I anywhere over the selected text and I changes to ▷.

- Insert Text
- Delete Text
- Undo Last Change
- **Move Text**
- Copy Text

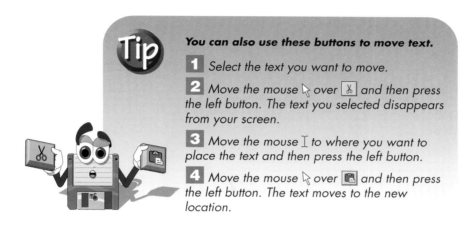

Tip

You can also use these buttons to move text.

1 Select the text you want to move.

2 Move the mouse ⌖ over ✂ and then press the left button. The text you selected disappears from your screen.

3 Move the mouse I to where you want to place the text and then press the left button.

4 Move the mouse ⌖ over 📋 and then press the left button. The text moves to the new location.

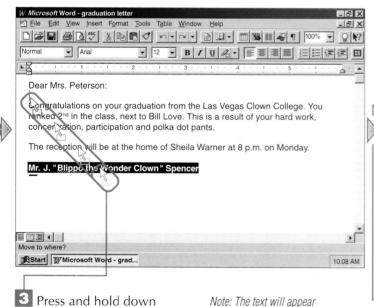

3 Press and hold down the left button as you drag the mouse ⇖ to where you want to place the text.

Note: The text will appear where you position the dotted insertion point on your screen.

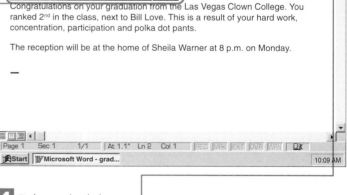

4 Release the left button and the text moves to the new location.

You can easily move the text back to its original location.

◆ To move the text back, move the mouse ⌖ over ↶ and then press the left button.

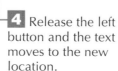

COPY TEXT

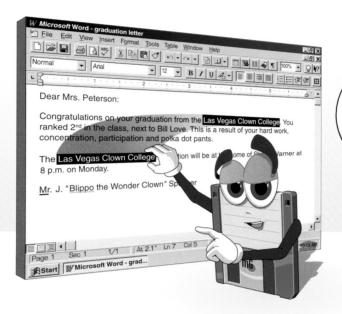

You can place a copy of text in a different location in your document. This will save you time, since you do not have to retype the text.

COPY TEXT

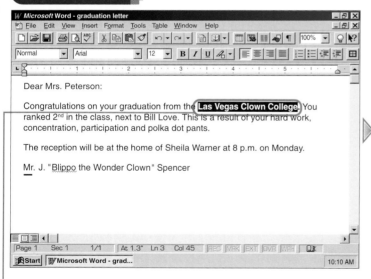

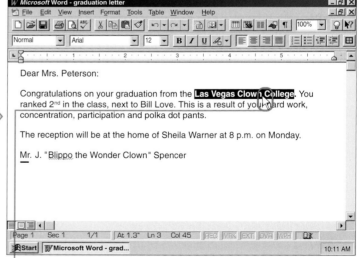

1 Select the text you want to copy.

Note: To select text, refer to page 10.

2 Move the mouse I anywhere over the selected text and I changes to $\text{\^{}}$.

3 Press and hold down Ctrl on your keyboard.

46

- Insert Text
- Delete Text
- Undo Last Change
- Move Text
- Copy Text

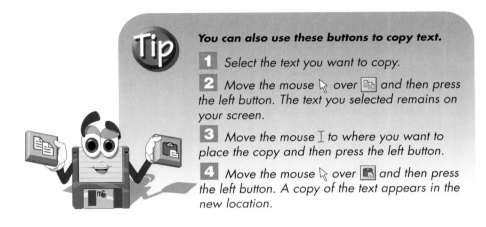

You can also use these buttons to copy text.

1 Select the text you want to copy.

2 Move the mouse ▷ over 🖹 and then press the left button. The text you selected remains on your screen.

3 Move the mouse Ⅰ to where you want to place the copy and then press the left button.

4 Move the mouse ▷ over 🖺 and then press the left button. A copy of the text appears in the new location.

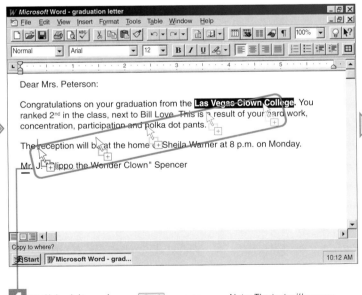

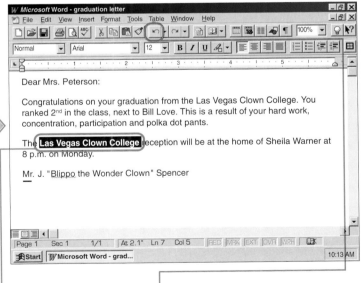

4 Still holding down Ctrl, press and hold down the left button as you drag the mouse ⬚ to where you want to place the copy.

Note: The text will appear where you position the dotted insertion point on your screen.

5 Release the left button and then release Ctrl.

◆ A copy of the text appears in the new location.

You can easily remove the copy of the text from your document.

◆ To remove the copy, move the mouse ▷ over ↩ and then press the left button.

SMART
EDITING

- Find Text
- Replace Text
- Spell Check One Word
- Spell Check Entire Document
- Using AutoText
- Using the Thesaurus
- Check Grammar

You can use the Find feature to locate a word or phrase in your document.

FIND TEXT

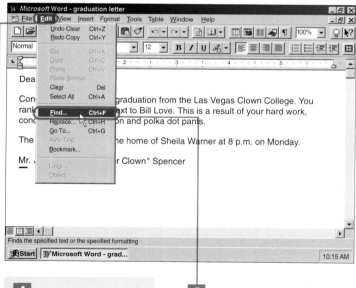

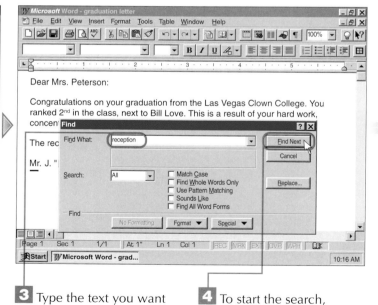

1 Move the mouse over **Edit** and then press the left button.

2 Move the mouse over **Find** and then press the left button.

◆ The **Find** dialog box appears.

3 Type the text you want to find (example: **reception**).

4 To start the search, move the mouse over **Find Next** and then press the left button.

- **Find Text**
- Replace Text
- Spell Check One Word
- Spell Check Entire Document

- Using AutoText
- Using the Thesaurus
- Check Grammar

Tip

You can end the search at any time by closing the Find dialog box.

◆ Move the mouse over **Cancel** and then press the left button.

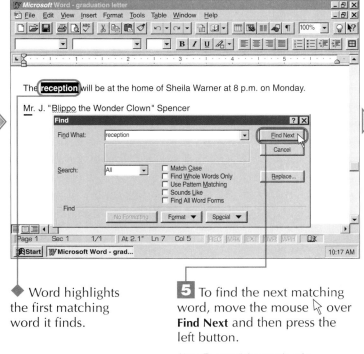

◆ Word highlights the first matching word it finds.

5 To find the next matching word, move the mouse ⌖ over **Find Next** and then press the left button.

Note: To cancel the search, refer to the Tip above.

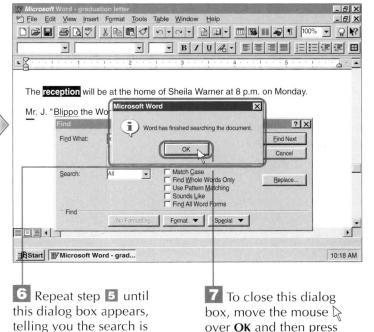

6 Repeat step **5** until this dialog box appears, telling you the search is complete.

7 To close this dialog box, move the mouse ⌖ over **OK** and then press the left button.

51

REPLACE TEXT

The Replace feature locates and replaces every occurrence of a word or phrase in your document. This is ideal if you have frequently misspelled a name.

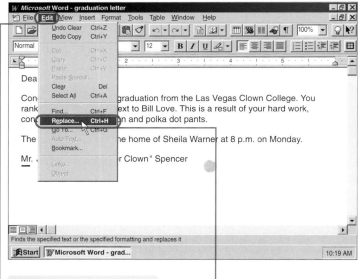

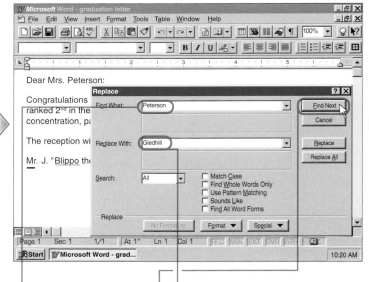

1 Move the mouse over **Edit** and then press the left button.

2 Move the mouse over **Replace** and then press the left button.

◆ The **Replace** dialog box appears.

3 Type the text you want to replace with new text (example: **Peterson**).

4 Press **Tab** on your keyboard to move to the **Replace With:** box. Then type the new text (example: **Gledhill**).

5 To start the search, move the mouse over **Find Next** and then press the left button.

- Find Text
- **Replace Text**
- Spell Check One Word
- Spell Check Entire Document
- Using AutoText
- Using the Thesaurus
- Check Grammar

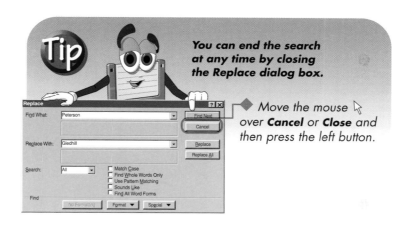

Tip

You can end the search at any time by closing the Replace dialog box.

◆ Move the mouse over **Cancel** or **Close** and then press the left button.

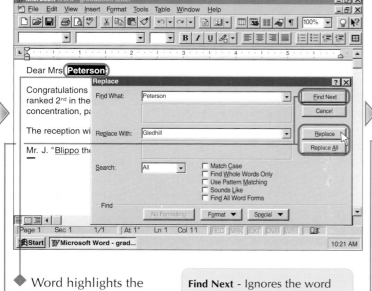

◆ Word highlights the first matching word it finds.

6 Move the mouse over one of these options and then press the left button.

Find Next - Ignores the word and searches for the next matching word.

Replace - Replaces the word and searches for the next matching word.

Replace All - Replaces the word and all other matching words in the document at once.

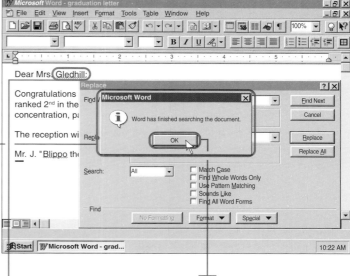

◆ In this example, Word replaces the text and searches for the next matching word.

7 Repeat step **6** until this dialog box appears, telling you the search is complete.

8 To close this dialog box, move the mouse over **OK** and then press the left button.

53

SPELL CHECK
ONE WORD

Word automatically checks your document for spelling errors as you type.

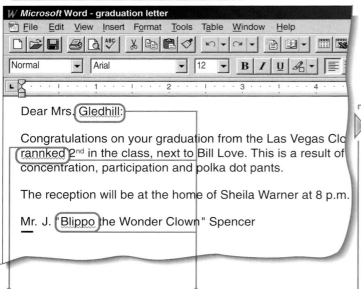

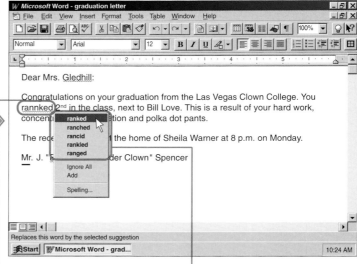

◆ In this example, the spelling of **ranked** was changed to **rannked**.

◆ Word displays a red line below every word it considers misspelled.

Note: These red lines will not appear when you print your document.

CORRECT MISSPELLED WORD

1 Move the mouse I anywhere over a word with a red underline and then press the **right** button. A menu appears.

2 To select the correct spelling, move the mouse ⊳ over the word and then press the left button.

Note: If Word does not display a spelling you want to use, move the mouse ⊳ outside the menu area and then press the left button.

54

- Find Text
- Replace Text
- **Spell Check One Word**
- Spell Check Entire Document
- Using AutoText
- Using the Thesaurus
- Check Grammar

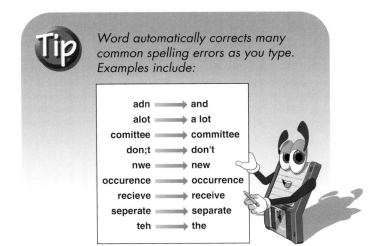

Tip

Word automatically corrects many common spelling errors as you type. Examples include:

adn	→	and
alot	→	a lot
comittee	→	committee
don;t	→	don't
nwe	→	new
occurence	→	occurrence
recieve	→	receive
seperate	→	separate
teh	→	the

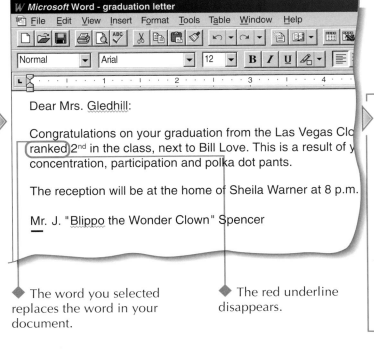

Dear Mrs. Gledhill:

Congratulations on your graduation from the Las Vegas Clo ranked 2nd in the class, next to Bill Love. This is a result of y concentration, participation and polka dot pants.

The reception will be at the home of Sheila Warner at 8 p.m.

Mr. J. "Blippo the Wonder Clown" Spencer

◆ The word you selected replaces the word in your document.

◆ The red underline disappears.

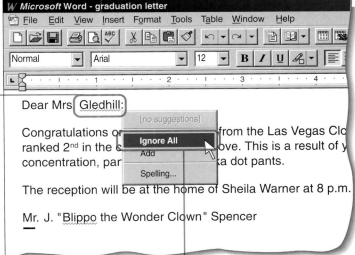

Dear Mrs Gledhill:

[no suggestions]

Ignore All

Add

Spelling...

Congratulations o from the Las Vegas Clo ranked 2nd in the c ove. This is a result of y concentration, par ka dot pants.

The reception will be at the home of Sheila Warner at 8 p.m.

Mr. J. "Blippo the Wonder Clown" Spencer

IGNORE MISSPELLED WORD

1 Move the mouse I anywhere over a word with a red underline and then press the **right** button. A menu appears.

2 To keep the spelling of the word and remove the red underline, move the mouse over **Ignore All** and then press the left button.

Note: Word will consider this word correctly spelled in all your documents until you exit the program.

SPELL CHECK ENTIRE DOCUMENT

You can use the Spelling feature to find and correct all the spelling errors in your document at once.

Word Dictionary

Word compares every word in your document to words in its dictionary. If a word does not exist in the dictionary, Word considers it misspelled.

Theery
Theory

SPELL CHECK ENTIRE DOCUMENT

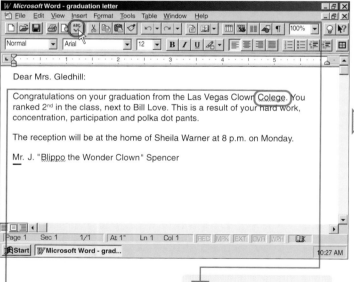

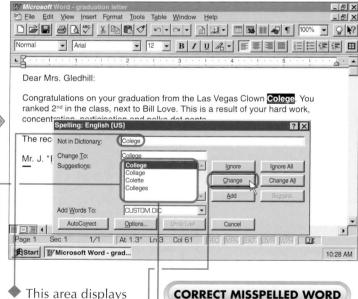

◆ In this example, the spelling of **College** was changed to **Colege**.

1 Move the mouse over [ABC] and then press the left button.

◆ The **Spelling** dialog box appears.

◆ This area displays the first word that is considered misspelled (example: **Colege**).

◆ The **Suggestions:** box displays alternative spellings.

CORRECT MISSPELLED WORD

2 To select the correct spelling, move the mouse over the word (example: **College**) and then press the left button.

3 Move the mouse over **Change** and then press the left button.

- Find Text
- Replace Text
- Spell Check One Word
- **Spell Check Entire Document**
- Using AutoText
- Using the Thesaurus
- Check Grammar

Tip

The Spelling feature will **not** find a correctly spelled word used in the wrong context.

You must review your document carefully to find this type of error.

The girl is sit years old

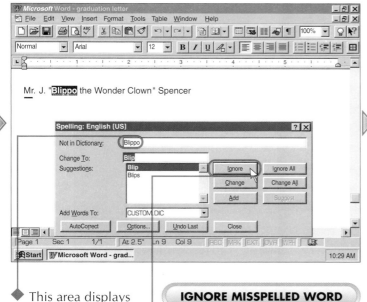

◆ This area displays the next word that is considered misspelled (example: **Blippo**).

IGNORE MISSPELLED WORD

4 To skip the word and continue checking your document, move the mouse ⌖ over **Ignore** and then press the left button.

*Note: To skip the word and all other occurrences of the word in your document, move the mouse ⌖ over **Ignore All** and then press the left button.*

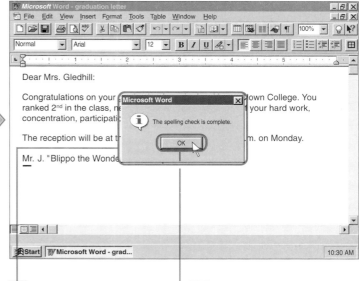

5 Correct or ignore misspelled words until this dialog box appears, telling you the spell check is complete.

6 To close the dialog box, move the mouse ⌖ over **OK** and then press the left button.

USING THE THESAURUS

You can use the Thesaurus to replace a word in your document with one that is more suitable.

entertaining guests
social gathering
dinner party
soirée
buffet luncheon
cocktail party
party
wake

USING THE THESAURUS

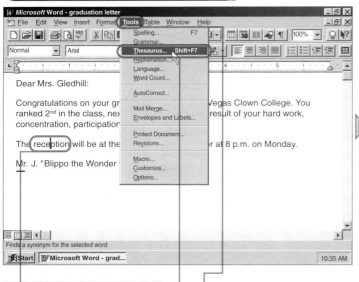

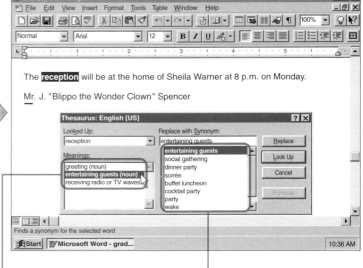

1 Move the mouse I anywhere over the word you want to look up (example: **reception**) and then press the left button.

2 Move the mouse over **Tools** and then press the left button.

3 Move the mouse over **Thesaurus** and then press the left button.

◆ The **Thesaurus** dialog box appears.

4 Move the mouse over the correct meaning of the word and then press the left button.

◆ This area displays words for the highlighted meaning. You can use one of these words to replace the word in your document.

- Find Text
- Replace Text
- Spell Check One Word
- Spell Check Entire Document

- Using AutoText
- **Using the Thesaurus**
- Check Grammar

Tip

Using the Thesaurus included with Word is faster and more convenient than searching through a printed thesaurus.

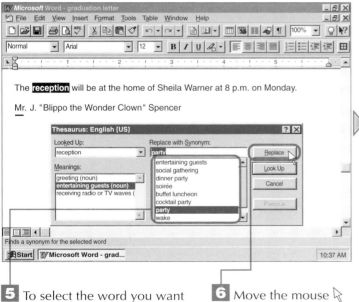

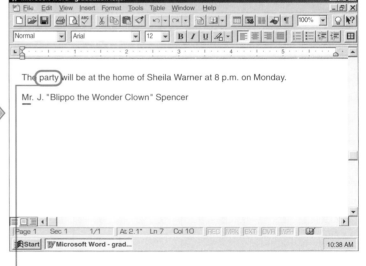

5 To select the word you want to use, move the mouse ⬚ over the word (example: **party**) and then press the left button.

*Note: If the Thesaurus does not offer a suitable replacement for the word in your document, move the mouse ⬚ over **Cancel** and then press the left button to close the dialog box.*

6 Move the mouse ⬚ over **Replace** and then press the left button.

◆ The word you selected replaces the word in your document.

You can use the Grammar feature to find and correct grammar, punctuation and stylistic errors in your document.

CHECK GRAMMAR

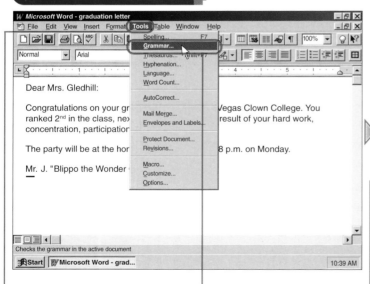

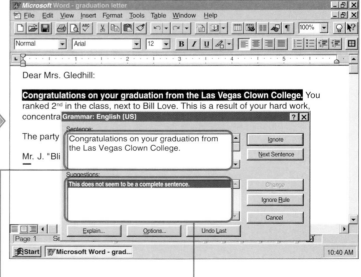

1 Move the mouse ☿ over **Tools** and then press the left button.

2 Move the mouse ☿ over **Grammar** and then press the left button.

*Note: If the **Grammar** option is not listed, you must install the Grammar feature to continue. To install the feature, refer to your Word 95 manual.*

◆ The **Grammar** dialog box appears.

◆ This area displays the first sentence containing an error.

◆ This area tells you what is wrong with the sentence and may offer a suggestion to correct the error.

- Find Text
- Replace Text
- Spell Check One Word
- Spell Check Entire Document

- Using AutoText
- Using the Thesaurus
- **Check Grammar**

Tip

Word also searches for spelling errors during a grammar check.

The **Spelling** dialog box appears if Word finds a spelling error in your document.

Note: For more information on correcting a spelling error, refer to page 56.

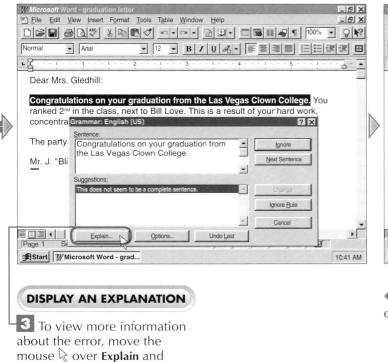

DISPLAY AN EXPLANATION

3 To view more information about the error, move the mouse ⌖ over **Explain** and then press the left button.

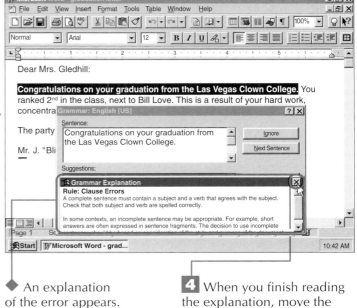

◆ An explanation of the error appears.

4 When you finish reading the explanation, move the mouse ⌖ over ✕ and then press the left button.

CONTINUED

63

The Grammar feature helps you improve the readability of your document.

CHECK GRAMMAR (CONTINUED)

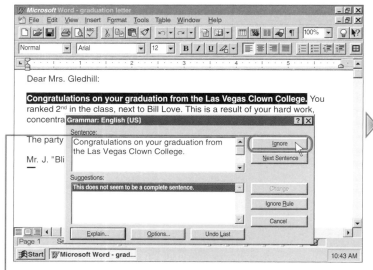

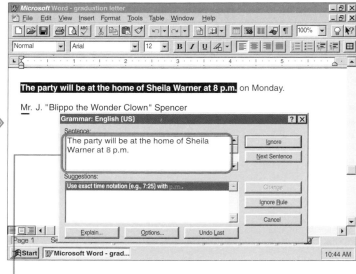

◆ This area displays the next sentence containing an error.

IGNORE AN ERROR

5 To ignore the error and continue checking your document, move the mouse over **Ignore** and then press the left button.

- Find Text
- Replace Text
- Spell Check One Word
- Spell Check Entire Document
- Using AutoText
- Using the Thesaurus
- **Check Grammar**

Tip

You can end the grammar check at any time by closing the Grammar dialog box.

◆ Move the mouse over **Cancel** and then press the left button.

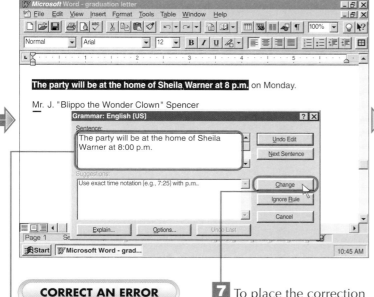

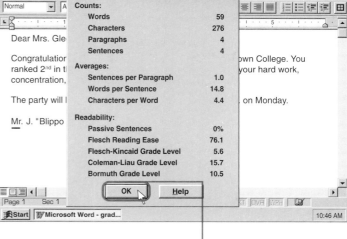

CORRECT AN ERROR

6 To correct the error, you can edit the text in this area (example: change **8** to **8:00**).

Note: To insert and delete text, refer to pages 38 to 40.

7 To place the correction in your document, move the mouse ⬚ over **Change** and then press the left button.

8 Ignore or correct grammatical errors until Word finishes checking your document.

◆ The **Readability Statistics** dialog box appears when the grammar check is complete.

9 To close the dialog box, move the mouse ⬚ over **OK** and then press the left button.

65

PRINT YOUR DOCUMENTS

Preview a Document

Print a Document

Print an Envelope

Print Labels

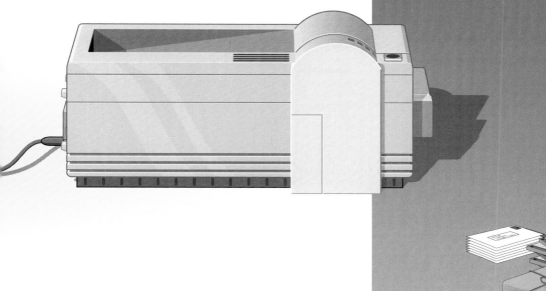

You can use Print Preview to see how your document will look when printed.

PREVIEW A DOCUMENT

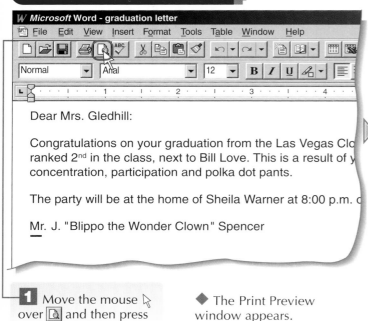

Dear Mrs. Gledhill:

Congratulations on your graduation from the Las Vegas Clo... ranked 2nd in the class, next to Bill Love. This is a result of y... concentration, participation and polka dot pants.

The party will be at the home of Sheila Warner at 8:00 p.m. o...

Mr. J. "Blippo the Wonder Clown" Spencer

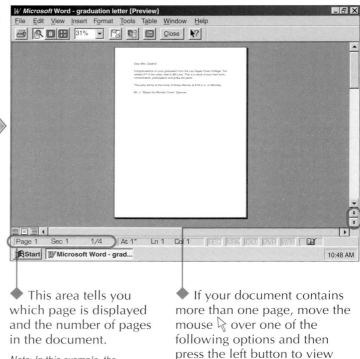

1 Move the mouse over [🔍] and then press the left button.

◆ The Print Preview window appears.

◆ This area tells you which page is displayed and the number of pages in the document.

Note: In this example, the document contains four pages.

◆ If your document contains more than one page, move the mouse over one of the following options and then press the left button to view another page.

[▲] Displays previous page.

[▼] Displays next page.

68

- **Preview a Document**
- Print a Document
- Print an Envelope
- Print Labels

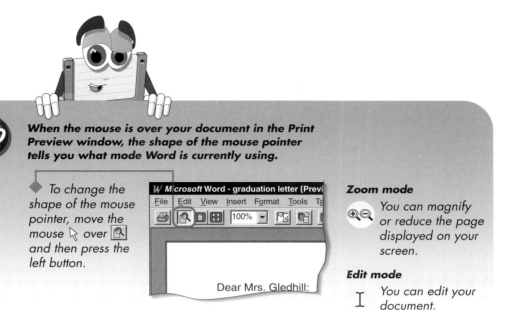

Tip

When the mouse is over your document in the Print Preview window, the shape of the mouse pointer tells you what mode Word is currently using.

◆ To change the shape of the mouse pointer, move the mouse ☖ over 🔍 and then press the left button.

Dear Mrs. Gledhill:

Zoom mode

You can magnify or reduce the page displayed on your screen.

Edit mode

I You can edit your document.

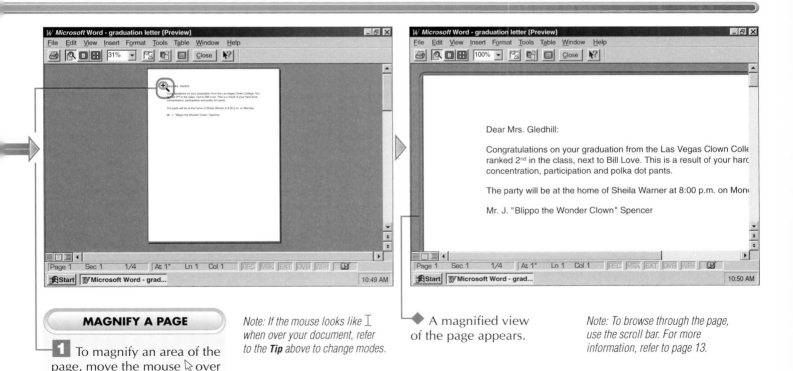

MAGNIFY A PAGE

1 To magnify an area of the page, move the mouse ☖ over the area (☖ changes to ⊕) and then press the left button.

*Note: If the mouse looks like I when over your document, refer to the **Tip** above to change modes.*

◆ A magnified view of the page appears.

Note: To browse through the page, use the scroll bar. For more information, refer to page 13.

69

In the Print Preview window, Word can display several pages at once. This lets you view the overall style of a long document.

PREVIEW A DOCUMENT

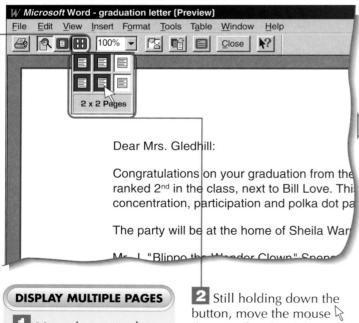

Dear Mrs. Gledhill:

Congratulations on your graduation from the ranked 2nd in the class, next to Bill Love. Thi concentration, participation and polka dot pa

The party will be at the home of Sheila War

Mr. L "Blippo the Wonder Clown" Spon

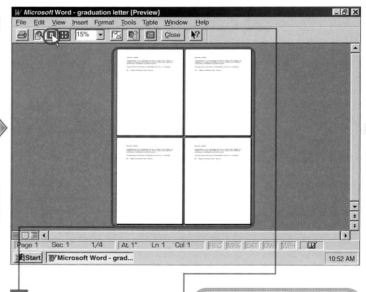

DISPLAY MULTIPLE PAGES

1 Move the mouse over 🔲 and then press and hold down the left button.

2 Still holding down the button, move the mouse down and to the right until you select the number of pages you want to display.

3 Release the button and the number of pages you specified appears on your screen.

Note: In this example, the document contains four pages.

DISPLAY ENTIRE PAGE

1 To display an entire page, move the mouse over 🔲 and then press the left button.

- **Preview a Document**   • Print an Envelope
- Print a Document   • Print Labels

Tip

SHRINK TO FIT

If the last page in your document contains only a few lines of text, Word can shrink the text to fit on one less page.

Move the mouse ⬧ over 🖼 in the Print Preview window and then press the left button.

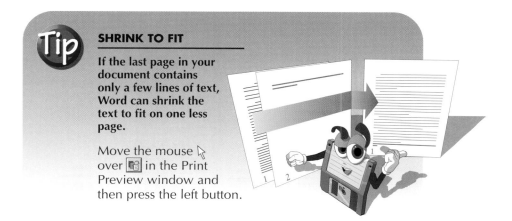

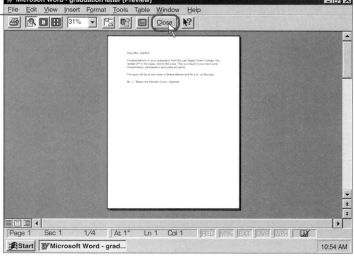

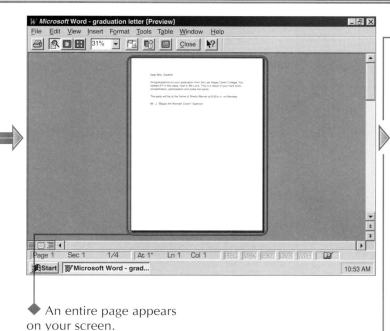

◆ An entire page appears on your screen.

CLOSE PRINT PREVIEW

1 To close the Print Preview window, move the mouse ⬧ over **Close** and then press the left button.

You can produce a paper copy of the document displayed on your screen.

PRINT A DOCUMENT

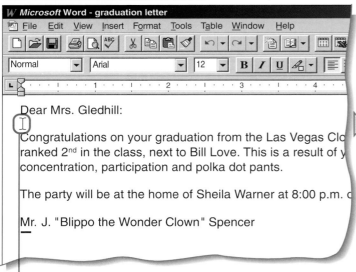

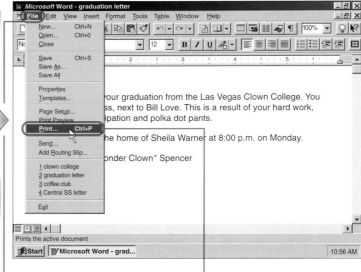

1 Move the mouse I anywhere over the document or page you want to print and then press the left button.

◆ To print a section of text, select the text.

Note: To select text, refer to page 10.

2 Move the mouse ⊳ over **File** and then press the left button.

3 Move the mouse ⊳ over **Print** and then press the left button.

◆ The **Print** dialog box appears.

PRINT SPECIFIC PAGES

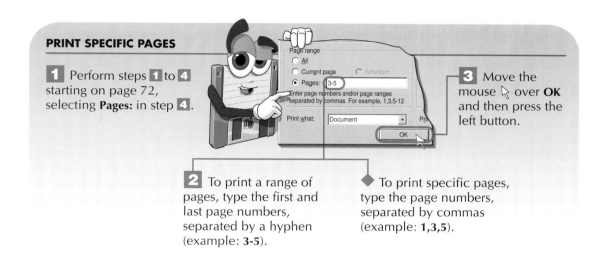

1 Perform steps **1** to **4** starting on page 72, selecting **Pages:** in step **4**.

3 Move the mouse 𝖐 over **OK** and then press the left button.

2 To print a range of pages, type the first and last page numbers, separated by a hyphen (example: **3-5**).

◆ To print specific pages, type the page numbers, separated by commas (example: **1,3,5**).

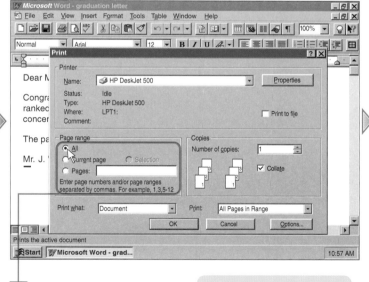

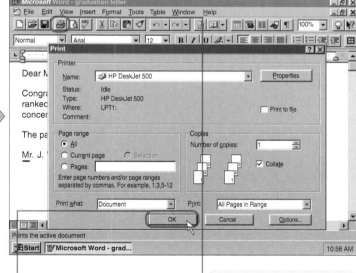

4 Move the mouse 𝖐 over the print option you want to use and then press the left button (○ changes to ◉).

All - Prints every page in the document.

Current page - Prints the page containing the insertion point.

Pages: - Prints the pages you specify.

Selection - Prints the text you selected.

5 Move the mouse 𝖐 over **OK** and then press the left button.

You can quickly print your entire document.

◆ Move the mouse 𝖐 over 🖨 and then press the left button.

You can easily print an address on an envelope.

PRINT AN ENVELOPE

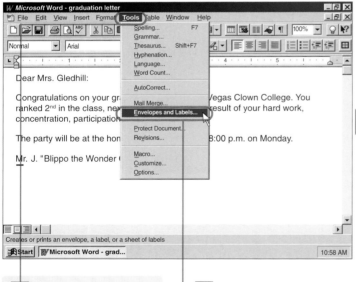

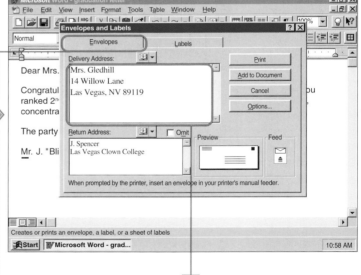

1 Move the mouse ⌖ over **Tools** and then press the left button.

2 Move the mouse ⌖ over **Envelopes and Labels** and then press the left button.

◆ The **Envelopes and Labels** dialog box appears.

3 Move the mouse ⌖ over the **Envelopes** tab and then press the left button.

4 To enter the delivery address, move the mouse ⌶ over this area and then press the left button. Then type the address.

Note: The area displays a delivery address if Word finds one in your document.

- Preview a Document
- Print a Document
- **Print an Envelope**
- Print Labels

A dialog box appears if you made changes to the return address in step 5 below.

◆ To save the changes, move the mouse ⇱ over **Yes** and then press the left button. The address will appear as the return address every time you print an envelope.

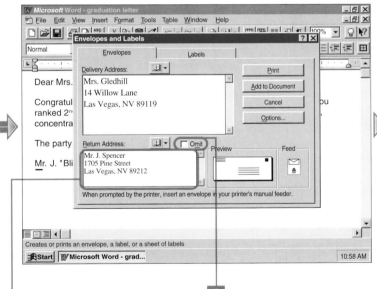

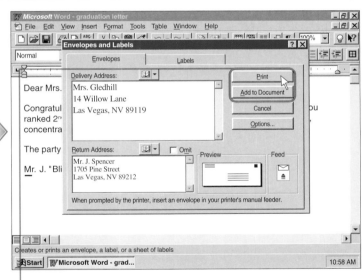

◆ This area displays a return address.

5 To enter a different return address, press **Tab** on your keyboard three times to highlight the existing address. Then type the address.

6 If you do not want to print a return address, move the mouse ⇱ over **Omit** and then press the left button (☐ changes to ☑).

Note: You can use the Omit option if your envelope already displays a return address. Company stationery often displays a return address.

7 Move the mouse ⇱ over one of the options and then press the left button.

Print - Prints the envelope.

Add to Document - Adds the envelope to the beginning of the document on your screen. This lets you save and print the envelope with the document.

You can easily print an address on labels.

PRINT LABELS

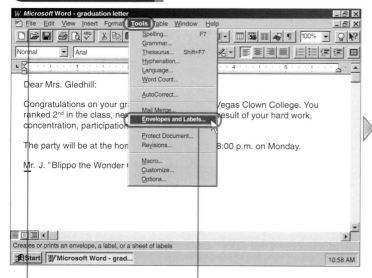

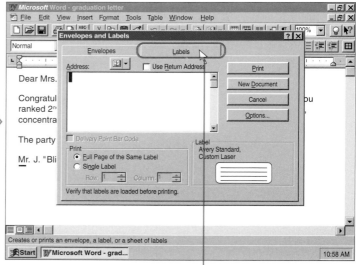

1 Move the mouse ⌖ over **Tools** and then press the left button.

2 Move the mouse ⌖ over **Envelopes and Labels** and then press the left button.

◆ The **Envelopes and Labels** dialog box appears.

3 Move the mouse ⌖ over the **Labels** tab and then press the left button.

- Preview a Document
- Print a Document
- Print an Envelope
- **Print Labels**

Tip

If you want to print a label for each customer on your mailing list, use the Merge feature.

Note: For information on using Merge to print labels, refer to page 200.

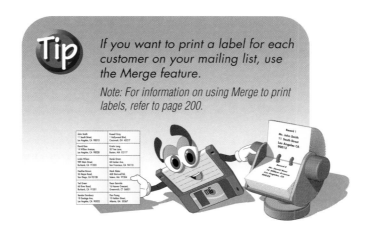

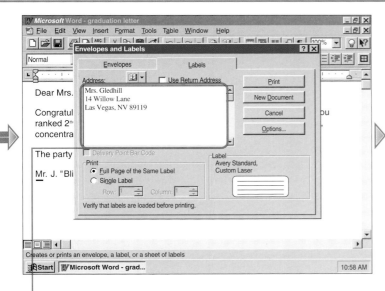

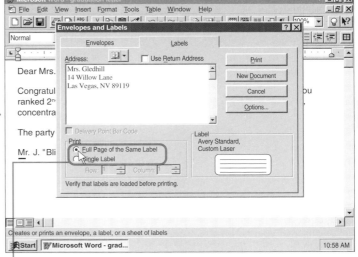

4 To enter the address you want to appear on the label(s), move the mouse I over the top of this area and then press the left button. Then type the address.

Note: The area displays an address if Word finds one in the document.

5 To specify the number of labels you want to print, move the mouse ⇗ over one of the options and then press the left button (○ changes to ◉).

Full Page of the Same Label - Prints the same address on every label on a page.

Single Label - Prints the address on only one label.

CONTINUED

77

Word offers many different label types and sizes.

HELLO
my name is...
Heather Brown

...Green
...Maple Road,
Las Vegas, NV 89119

Mrs. Gledhill
...4 Willow Lane
...Las Vegas, NV 89119

PRINT LABELS (CONTINUED)

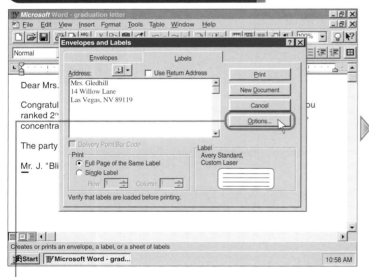

6 To change the type of label you want to use, move the mouse ⓚ over **Options** and then press the left button.

◆ The **Label Options** dialog box appears.

7 Move the mouse ⓚ over the type of label you want to use and then press the left button. To select the correct type of label, refer to the label packaging.

Note: To view all the available labels, use the scroll bar. For more information, refer to page 13.

- Preview a Document
- Print a Document
- Print an Envelope
- **Print Labels**

Tip

You can use labels for envelopes, packages, file folders, diskettes, video cassettes, name tags and index cards.

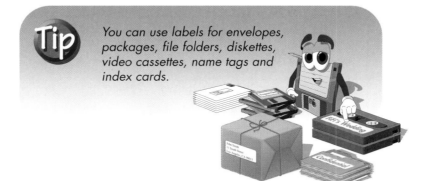

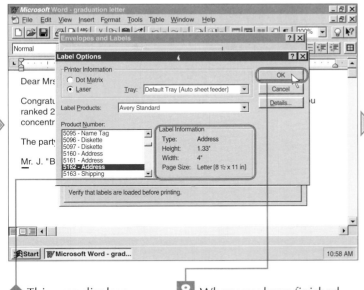

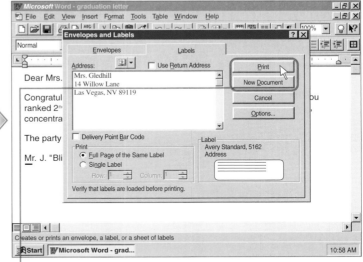

◆ This area displays information about the type of label you selected.

8 When you have finished selecting the type of label, move the mouse ⬚ over **OK** and then press the left button.

9 To print the label(s), move the mouse ⬚ over one of the options and then press the left button.

Print - Prints the label(s).

New Document - Creates a document that you can save and print as you would any document.

Note: The New Document option is not available if you selected **Single Label** in step **5** on page 77.

79

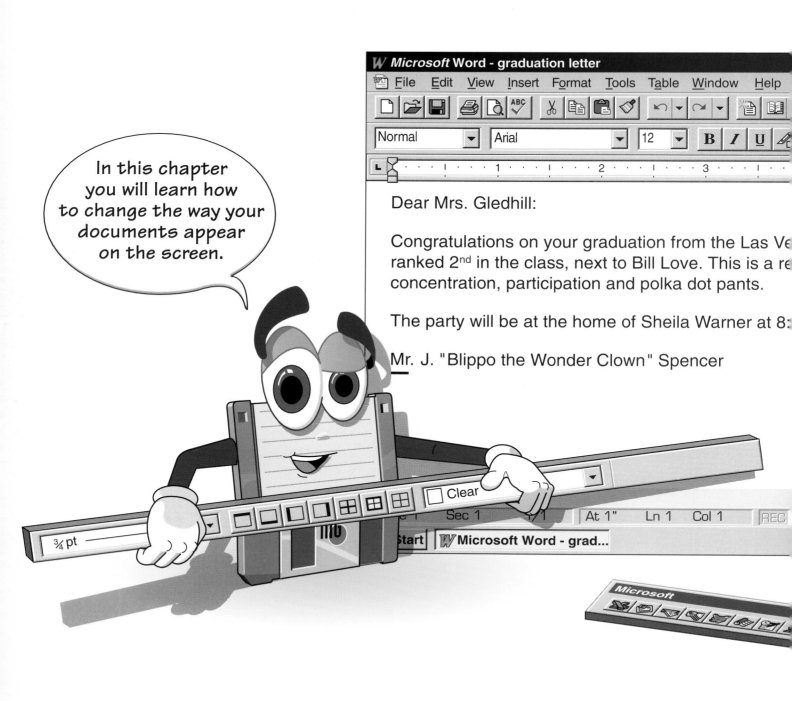

CHANGE YOUR DOCUMENT DISPLAY

Change Views

Zoom In or Out

Hide or Display the Ruler

Hide or Display Toolbars

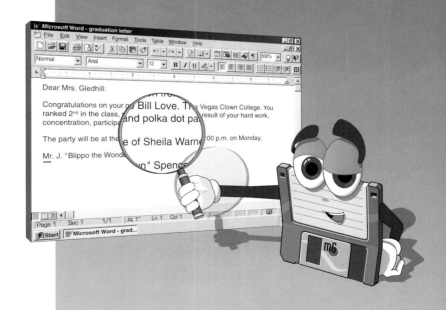

ZOOM IN OR OUT

HIDE OR DISPLAY THE RULER

> Word lets you enlarge or reduce the display of text on your screen.

● You can magnify the document to read small text.

● You can reduce the document to display more text on your screen.

ZOOM IN OR OUT

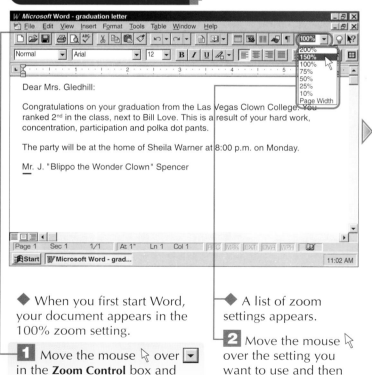

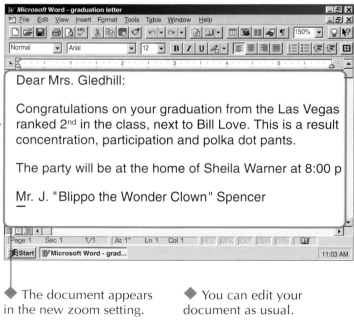

◆ When you first start Word, your document appears in the 100% zoom setting.

1 Move the mouse ⌖ over ▼ in the **Zoom Control** box and then press the left button.

◆ A list of zoom settings appears.

2 Move the mouse ⌖ over the setting you want to use and then press the left button.

◆ The document appears in the new zoom setting.

◆ You can edit your document as usual.

Note: To return to the normal zoom setting, repeat steps 1 and 2, selecting 100% in step 2.

- Change Views
- **Zoom In or Out**
- **Hide or Display the Ruler**
- Hide or Display Toolbars

You can use the ruler to position text and graphics on a page. You can hide or display the ruler at any time.

Hiding the ruler provides a larger and less cluttered working area.

HIDE OR DISPLAY THE RULER

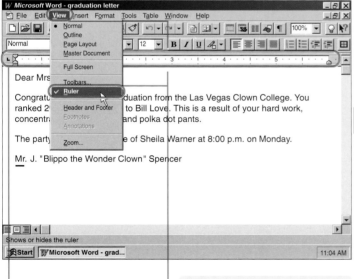

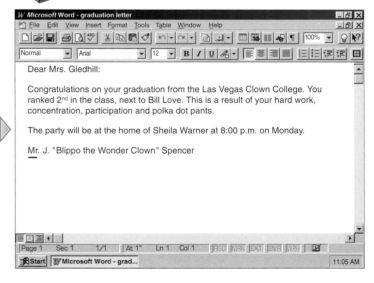

◆ When you first start Word, the ruler is displayed on your screen.

1 To hide the ruler, move the mouse ℞ over **View** and then press the left button.

2 Move the mouse ℞ over **Ruler** and then press the left button.

◆ Word hides the ruler.

*Note: To redisplay the ruler, repeat steps **1** and **2**.*

HIDE OR DISPLAY TOOLBARS

> Word offers several toolbars that you can hide or display at any time. Each toolbar contains a series of buttons that let you quickly select commands.

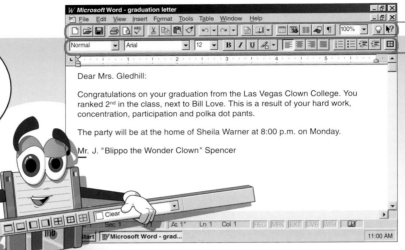

Standard

Formatting

When you first start Word, the Standard and Formatting toolbars appear on your screen.

HIDE OR DISPLAY TOOLBARS

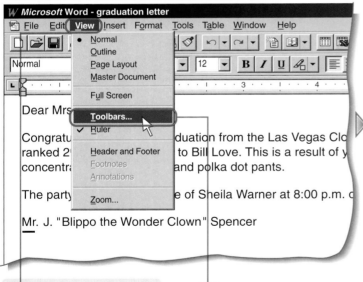

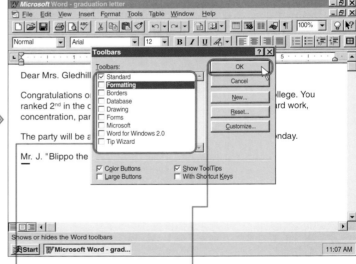

1 Move the mouse ⬆ over **View** and then press the left button.

2 Move the mouse ⬆ over **Toolbars** and then press the left button.

◆ The **Toolbars** dialog box appears.

3 Move the mouse ⬆ over the name of the toolbar you want to hide or display and then press the left button.

☐ The toolbar will not appear on your screen.

☑ The toolbar will appear on your screen.

4 Repeat step **3** until you select all the toolbars you want to hide or display.

5 Move the mouse ⬆ over **OK** and then press the left button.

86

- Change Views
- Zoom In or Out
- Hide or Display the Ruler
- **Hide or Display Toolbars**

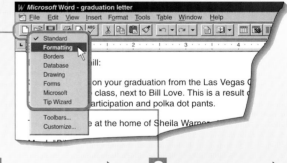

Tip

A screen displaying fewer toolbars provides a larger and less cluttered working area.

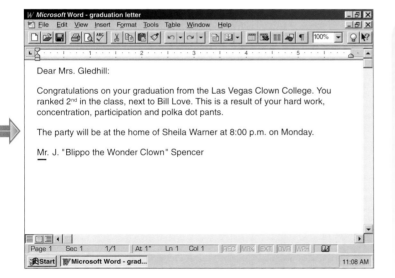

◆ Word hides or displays the toolbar(s) you selected.

You can quickly hide or display a toolbar.

 1 Move the mouse anywhere over a toolbar displayed on your screen and then press the **right** button. A list of toolbar names appears.

2 Move the mouse over the name of the toolbar you want to display or hide and then press the left button.

Note: A check mark (✓) beside a toolbar name tells you the toolbar is currently displayed on your screen.

USING MULTIPLE DOCUMENTS

Create a New Document

Switch Between Documents

Arrange Open Documents

Maximize a Document

Copy or Move Text Between Documents

Minimize the Word Screen

Close a Document

You can create a document to start a new letter, report or memo.

CREATE A NEW DOCUMENT

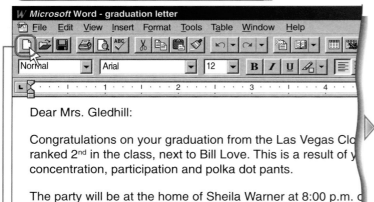

1 Move the mouse ℝ over 🗋 and then press the left button.

◆ A new document appears.

Note: The previous document is now hidden behind the new document.

◆ Think of each document as a separate piece of paper. When you create a document, you are placing a new piece of paper on your screen.

- **Create a New Document**
- **Switch Between Documents**
- Arrange Open Documents
- Maximize a Document
- Copy or Move Text Between Documents
- Minimize the Word Screen
- Close a Document

Word lets you have many documents open at once. You can easily switch between all your open documents.

SWITCH BETWEEN DOCUMENTS

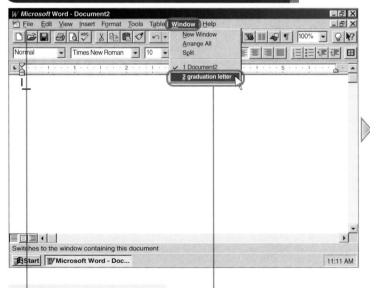

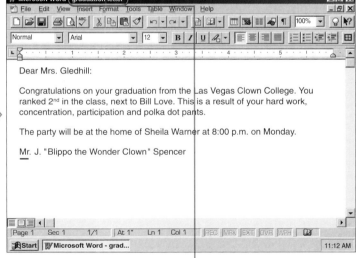

1 To display a list of all your open documents, move the mouse ⌕ over **Window** and then press the left button.

2 Move the mouse ⌕ over the document you want to display and then press the left button.

◆ The document appears.

◆ Word displays the name of the document at the top of your screen.

91

ARRANGE OPEN DOCUMENTS

MAXIMIZE A DOCUMENT

If you have several documents open, some of them may be hidden. You can use the Arrange All command to display the contents of all your open documents.

ARRANGE OPEN DOCUMENTS

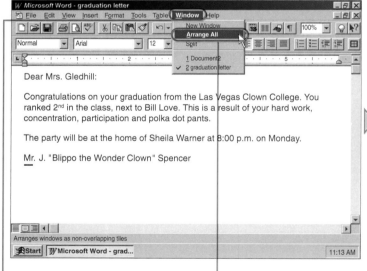

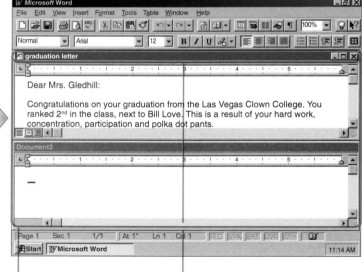

1 Move the mouse ℝ over **Window** and then press the left button.

2 Move the mouse ℝ over **Arrange All** and then press the left button.

◆ You can now view the contents of all your open documents.

◆ You can only work in the current document, which displays a highlighted title bar.

Note: To make another document current, move the mouse ℝ anywhere over the document and then press the left button.

- Create a New Document
- Switch Between Documents
- **Arrange Open Documents**
- **Maximize a Document**
- Copy or Move Text Between Documents
- Minimize the Word Screen
- Close a Document

> You can enlarge a document to fill your screen. This lets you view more of its contents.

MAXIMIZE A DOCUMENT

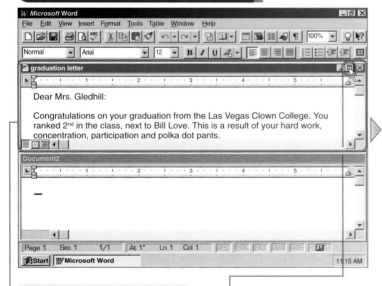

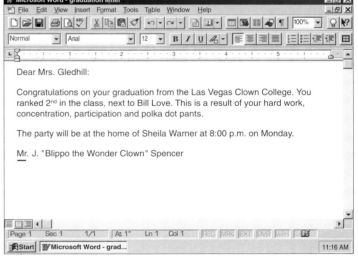

1 To select the document you want to maximize, move the mouse ⌖ over the document and then press the left button.

2 Move the mouse ⌖ over ▣ and then press the left button.

◆ The document fills your screen.

Note: The maximized document covers all your open documents.

93

COPY OR MOVE TEXT BETWEEN DOCUMENTS

> Copying or moving text between documents saves you time when you are working in one document and want to use text from another.

COPY OR MOVE TEXT BETWEEN DOCUMENTS

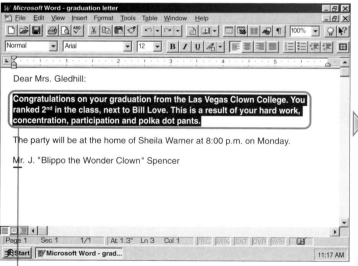

Dear Mrs. Gledhill:

Congratulations on your graduation from the Las Vegas Clown College. You ranked 2nd in the class, next to Bill Love. This is a result of your hard work, concentration, participation and polka dot pants.

The party will be at the home of Sheila Warner at 8:00 p.m. on Monday.

Mr. J. "Blippo the Wonder Clown" Spencer

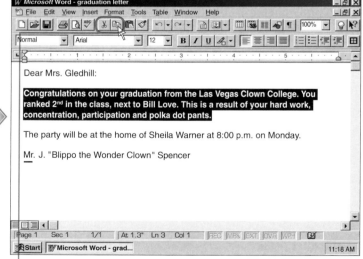

Dear Mrs. Gledhill:

Congratulations on your graduation from the Las Vegas Clown College. You ranked 2nd in the class, next to Bill Love. This is a result of your hard work, concentration, participation and polka dot pants.

The party will be at the home of Sheila Warner at 8:00 p.m. on Monday.

Mr. J. "Blippo the Wonder Clown" Spencer

1 Select the text you want to place in another document.

Note: To select text, refer to page 10.

2 Move the mouse ⤒ over one of the following options and then press the left button.

✂ Moves the text.

⧉ Copies the text.

94

- Create a New Document
- Switch Between Documents
- Arrange Open Documents
- Maximize a Document
- Copy or Move Text Between Documents
- Minimize the Word Screen
- Close a Document

The Copy and Move features both place text in a new location, but they have one distinct difference.

COPY TEXT

When you copy text, the original text remains in its place.

MOVE TEXT

When you move text, the original text disappears.

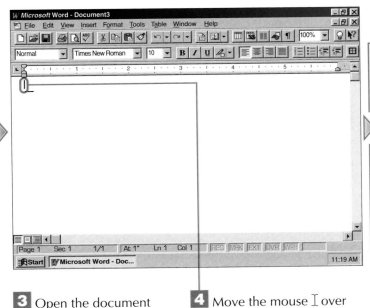

3 Open the document where you want to place the text.

Note: To create a new document, refer to page 90. To open a saved document, refer to page 28.

4 Move the mouse I over the location in the document where you want to place the text and then press the left button.

5 Move the mouse ⬚ over 🖹 and then press the left button.

◆ The text appears in the document.

If you need to perform another task in Windows, you can remove Word from your screen without exiting the program. You can then quickly redisplay Word at any time.

MINIMIZE THE WORD SCREEN

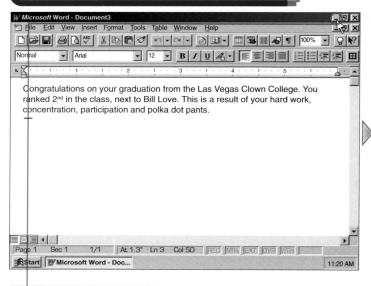

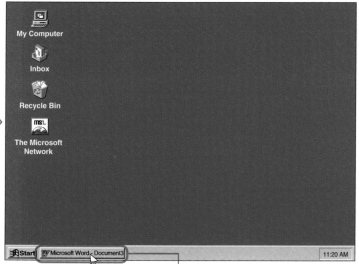

1 Move the mouse ▷ over 🔲 and then press the left button.

◆ The Word screen disappears.

2 To redisplay the Word document, move the mouse ▷ over its button at the bottom of your screen and then press the left button.

- Create a New Document
- Switch Between Documents
- Arrange Open Documents
- Maximize a Document

- Copy or Move Text Between Documents
- **Minimize the Word Screen**
- **Close a Document**

> When you finish working with a document, you can close the document to remove it from your screen.

CLOSE A DOCUMENT

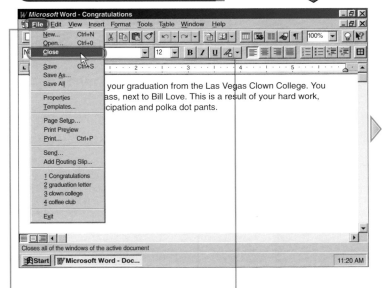

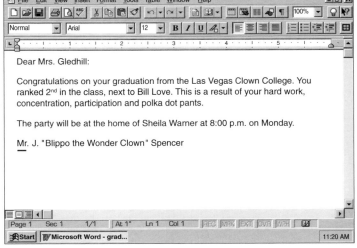

◆ To save the document before closing, refer to page 22.

1 To close the document displayed on your screen, move the mouse over **File** and then press the left button.

2 Move the mouse over **Close** and then press the left button.

◆ Word removes the document from your screen.

Note: If you had more than one document open, the second last document you worked on appears on your screen.

You can use the Bold, Italic and Underline features to emphasize information in your document.

Bold   *Italic*   <u>Underline</u>

BOLD, ITALIC AND UNDERLINE

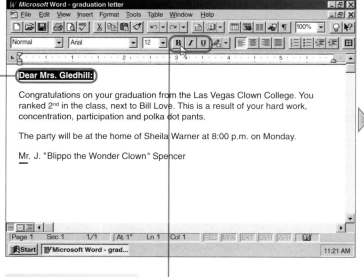

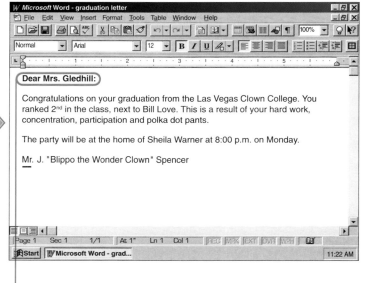

1 Select the text you want to change.

Note: To select text, refer to page 10.

2 Move the mouse ⌖ over one of the following options and then press the left button.

B Bold text

I Italicize text

<u>U</u> Underline text

◆ The text you selected appears in the new style.

Note: To deselect text, move the mouse ⏉ outside the selected area and then press the left button.

◆ To remove a bold, italic or underline style, repeat steps **1** and **2**.

100

You can increase or decrease the size of text in your document.

8 point
12 point
14 point
18 point
24 point

Word measures the size of text in points. There are approximately 72 points in one inch.

- Smaller text lets you fit more information on a page.

- Larger text is easier to read.

CHANGE SIZE OF TEXT

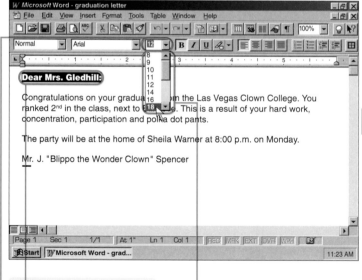

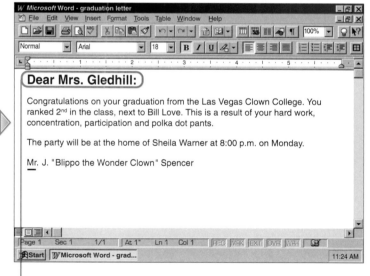

1 Select the text you want to change.

2 To display a list of the available sizes, move the mouse ⬚ over ▾ in this area and then press the left button.

3 Move the mouse ⬚ over the size you want to use (example: **18**) and then press the left button.

Note: To view all the available sizes, use the scroll bar. For more information, refer to page 13.

◆ The text you selected changes to the new size.

Note: To deselect text, move the mouse I outside the selected area and then press the left button.

CHANGE FONTS

You can enhance the appearance of your document by changing the design of characters.

CHANGE DESIGN OF TEXT

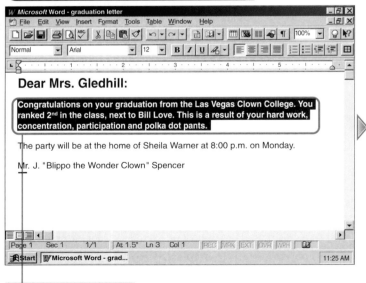

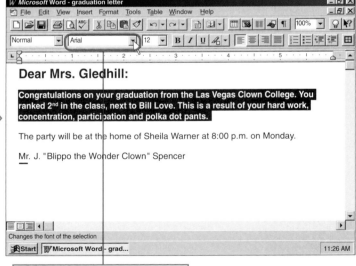

1 Select the text you want to change.

Note: To select text, refer to page 10.

◆ This area displays the current font of the text you selected.

2 To display a list of the available fonts, move the mouse ⓘ over ▾ in this area and then press the left button.

- Bold, Italic and Underline
- **Change Fonts**
- Use Format Painter
- Highlight Text
- Insert Symbols

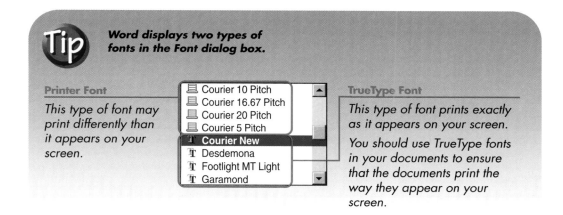

Tip *Word displays two types of fonts in the Font dialog box.*

Printer Font

This type of font may print differently than it appears on your screen.

| Courier 10 Pitch |
| Courier 16.67 Pitch |
| Courier 20 Pitch |
| Courier 5 Pitch |
| **Courier New** |
| Desdemona |
| Footlight MT Light |
| Garamond |

TrueType Font

This type of font prints exactly as it appears on your screen.

You should use TrueType fonts in your documents to ensure that the documents print the way they appear on your screen.

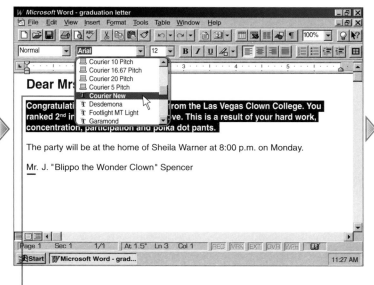

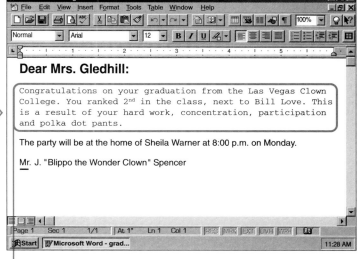

3 Move the mouse ⬚ over the font you want to use (example: **Courier New**) and then press the left button.

Note: To view all the available fonts, use the scroll bar. For more information, refer to page 13.

◆ The text you selected changes to the new font.

Note: To deselect text, move the mouse ⊥ outside the selected area and then press the left button.

CHANGE FONTS

You can change the design and size of characters in your document at the same time.

CHANGE FONT OF TEXT

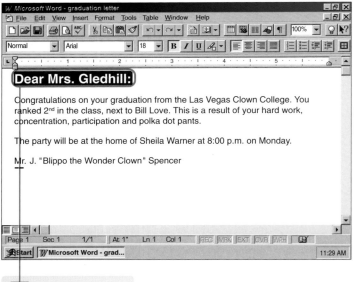

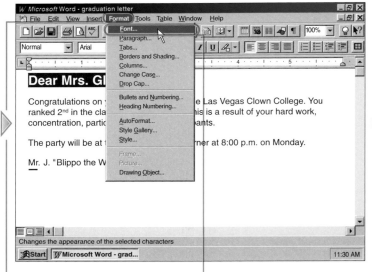

1 Select the text you want to change.

Note: To select text, refer to page 10.

2 Move the mouse over **Format** and then press the left button.

3 Move the mouse over **Font** and then press the left button.

◆ The **Font** dialog box appears.

- Bold, Italic and Underline
- Change Fonts
- Use Format Painter
- Highlight Text
- Insert Symbols

Tip

The fonts available on your computer may be different from the fonts on other computers. The available fonts depend on your printer and the setup of your computer.

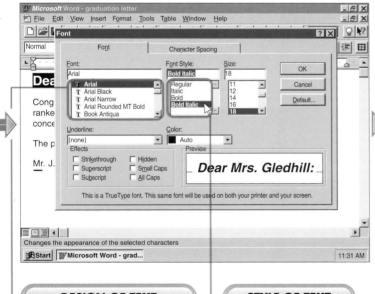

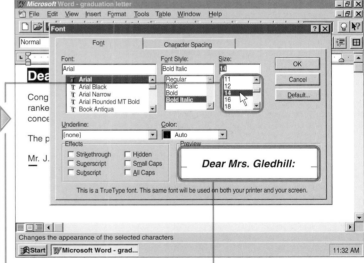

DESIGN OF TEXT

4 To change the design of the text, move the mouse ⬡ over the font you want to use (example: **Arial**) and then press the left button.

*Note: To view more options in the **Font** dialog box, use the scroll bars. For more information, refer to page 13.*

STYLE OF TEXT

5 To change the style of the text, move the mouse ⬡ over the style you want to use (example: **Bold Italic**) and then press the left button.

SIZE OF TEXT

6 To change the size of the text, move the mouse ⬡ over the size you want to use (example: **14**) and then press the left button.

◆ This area displays a preview of all the options you have selected.

CONTINUED

105

CHANGE FONTS

You can easily select an underline style or add special effects to text in your document.

Underline Styles

<u>Single Underline</u>

<u>Words</u> <u>Only</u>

<u>Double Underline</u>

<u>Dotted</u>

Effects

~~Strikethrough~~

Text superscript

Text subscript

SMALL CAPS

ALL CAPS

CHANGE FONT OF TEXT (CONTINUED)

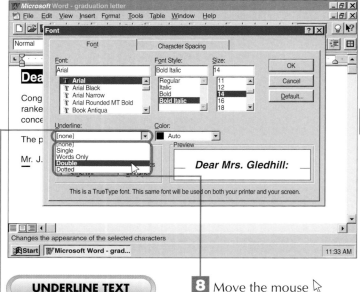

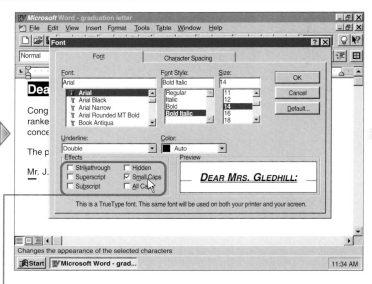

UNDERLINE TEXT

7 To select an underline style, move the mouse over this area and then press the left button.

8 Move the mouse over the underline style you want to use (example: **Double**) and then press the left button.

TEXT EFFECTS

9 To select a text effect, move the mouse over the effect you want to use and then press the left button (☐ changes to ☑).

Note: To turn off an effect, move the mouse over the effect and then press the left button (☑ changes to ☐).

106

- Bold, Italic and Underline
- **Change Fonts**
- Use Format Painter

- Highlight Text
- Insert Symbols

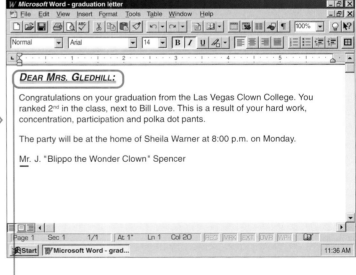

Tip

You can instantly remove all character formats from text in your document.

1 Select the text displaying the formats you want to remove.

2 Press and hold down `Ctrl` and then press the **Spacebar** on your keyboard. Then release the keys.

Dear Mrs. Gledhill:

Congratulations on your graduation from the Las Vegas Clown College. You ranked 2nd in the class, next to Bill Love. This is a result of your hard work, concentration, participation and polka dot pants.

The party will be at the home of Sheila Warner at 8:00 p.m. on Monday.

Mr. J. "Blippo the Wonder Clown" Spencer

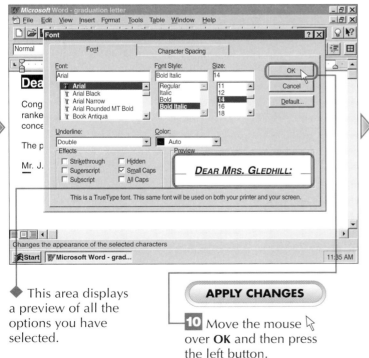

◆ This area displays a preview of all the options you have selected.

APPLY CHANGES

10 Move the mouse ⬚ over **OK** and then press the left button.

◆ The text you selected displays the changes.

Note: To deselect text, move the mouse I outside the selected area and then press the left button.

USE FORMAT PAINTER

If you like the appearance of an area of text, you can make another area of text look exactly the same.

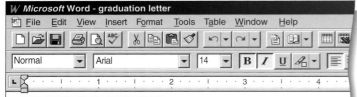

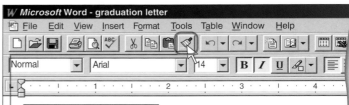

1 Select the text that displays the formats you like.

Note: To select text, refer to page 10.

2 Move the mouse over and then quickly press the left button twice.

- Bold, Italic and Underline
- Change Fonts
- **Use Format Painter**
- Highlight Text
- Insert Symbols

Tip

You can use the AutoFormat feature to instantly give your entire document a consistent look.

Note: For more information on the AutoFormat feature, refer to page 143.

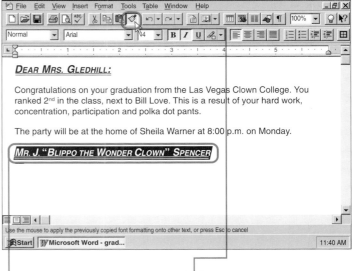

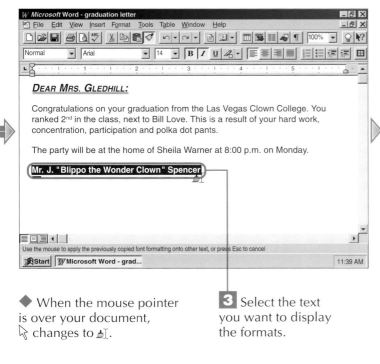

◆ When the mouse pointer is over your document, ⌖ changes to 🖌I.

3 Select the text you want to display the formats.

◆ When you release the left button, the text you selected displays the formats.

4 Repeat step **3** until you have selected all the text you want to display the formats.

5 When you have finished, move the mouse ⌖ over 🖌 and then press the left button.

You can highlight important text in your document.

HIGHLIGHT TEXT

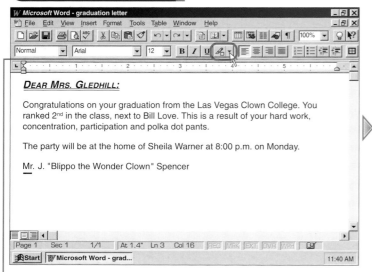

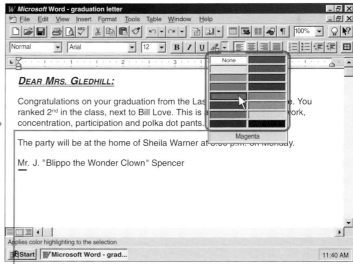

1 To select a color for the highlight, move the mouse ⌖ over ⬝ and then press and hold down the left button.

2 Still holding down the button, drag the mouse ⌖ down and to the right to display all the available colors. Move the mouse ⌖ over the color you want to use and then release the button.

- Bold, Italic and Underline
- Change Fonts
- Use Format Painter
- **Highlight Text**
- Insert Symbols

Tip

The Highlight feature is useful for marking text you want to verify later.

The college expects a total enrollment of 952 students for the upcoming school year. This number represents an 8 per cent increase over last year.

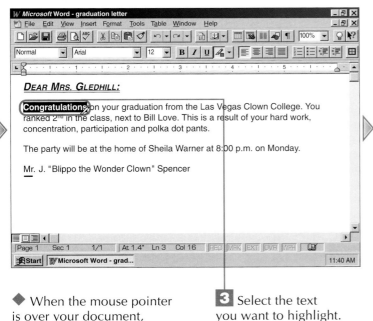

◆ When the mouse pointer is over your document, ⊿ changes to ⊿ .

3 Select the text you want to highlight.

Note: To select text, refer to page 10.

◆ When you release the left button, the text you selected displays the highlight.

4 Repeat step **3** until you have selected all the text you want to highlight.

5 When you have finished, move the mouse ⊿ over ⊿ and then press the left button.

*Note: To remove a highlight, repeat steps **1** to **5**, selecting **None** in step **2**.*

INSERT SYMBOLS

You can insert symbols into your document that do not appear on your keyboard.

INSERT SYMBOLS

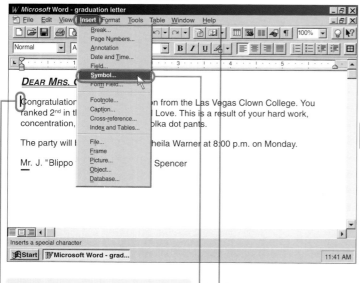

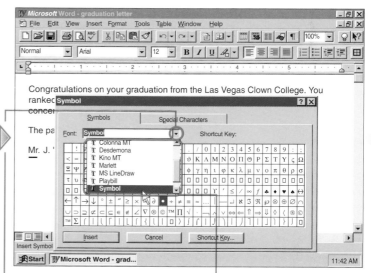

1 Move the mouse I to where you want a symbol to appear in your document and then press the left button.

2 Move the mouse Ⓚ over **Insert** and then press the left button.

3 Move the mouse ⓀK over **Symbol** and then press the left button.

◆ The **Symbol** dialog box appears, displaying the current set of symbols.

4 To display another set of symbols, move the mouse ⓀK over ▾ and then press the left button.

5 Move the mouse ⓀK over the set of symbols you want to use and then press the left button.

Note: To view all the available sets of symbols, use the scroll bar. For more information, refer to page 13.

- Bold, Italic and Underline
- Change Fonts
- Use Format Painter

- Highlight Text
- **Insert Symbols**

Tip

If you type one of the following sets of characters, Word will instantly replace the characters with a symbol. This lets you quickly enter symbols that are not available on your keyboard.

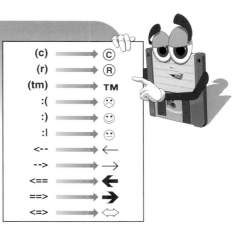

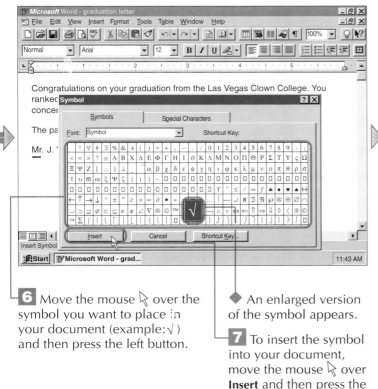

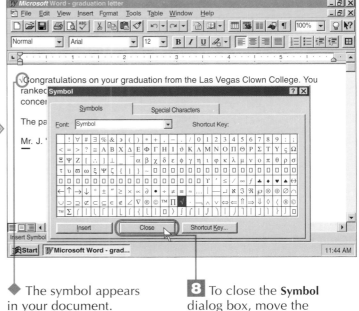

6 Move the mouse ⊳ over the symbol you want to place in your document (example: √) and then press the left button.

◆ An enlarged version of the symbol appears.

7 To insert the symbol into your document, move the mouse ⊳ over **Insert** and then press the left button.

◆ The symbol appears in your document.

8 To close the **Symbol** dialog box, move the mouse ⊳ over **Close** and then press the left button.

CHANGE LINE SPACING

You can make your document easier to read by changing the amount of space between the lines of text.

Single
1.5 Lines
Double

CHANGE LINE SPACING

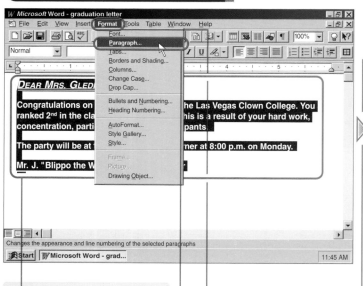

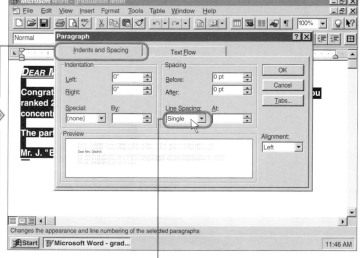

1 Select the paragraph(s) you want to change to a new line spacing.

Note: To select text, refer to page 10.

2 Move the mouse ℞ over **Format** and then press the left button.

3 Move the mouse ℞ over **Paragraph** and then press the left button.

◆ The **Paragraph** dialog box appears.

4 Move the mouse ℞ over the **Indents and Spacing** tab and then press the left button.

◆ This area displays the line spacing for the selected paragraph(s).

5 To display a list of the available line spacing options, move the mouse ℞ over this area and then press the left button.

- **Change Line Spacing**
- Indent a Paragraph
- Change Paragraph Alignment
- Add Bullets or Numbers
- Change Tab Settings
- Add Borders
- Add Shading

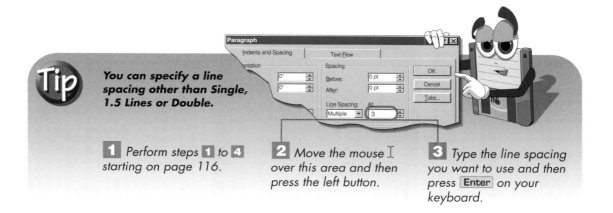

Tip

You can specify a line spacing other than Single, 1.5 Lines or Double.

1 Perform steps **1** to **4** starting on page 116.

2 Move the mouse I over this area and then press the left button.

3 Type the line spacing you want to use and then press **Enter** on your keyboard.

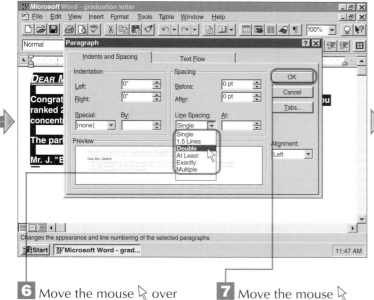

6 Move the mouse � over the line spacing option you want to use (example: **Double**) and then press the left button.

7 Move the mouse � over **OK** and then press the left button.

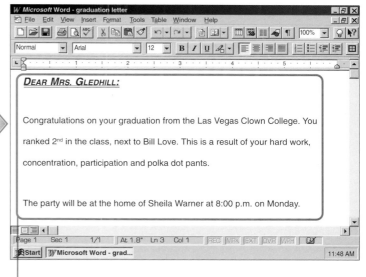

◆ Word changes the line spacing of the paragraph(s) you selected.

Note: To deselect text, move the mouse I outside the selected area and then press the left button.

INDENT A PARAGRAPH

You can use the Indent feature to emphasize paragraphs in your document.

INDENT A PARAGRAPH

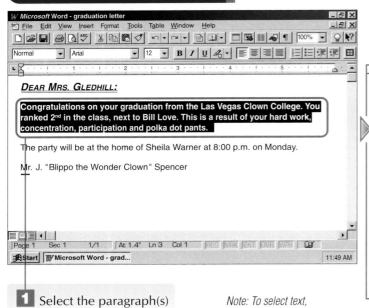

1 Select the paragraph(s) you want to indent.

Note: To select text, refer to page 10.

2 Move the mouse over one of the indent symbols (example:) and then press and hold down the left button.

3 Still holding down the button, drag the mouse to where you want to place the symbol.

◆ A line shows the new indent position.

- Change Line Spacing
- **Indent a Paragraph**
- Change Paragraph Alignment
- Add Bullets or Numbers
- Change Tab Settings
- Add Borders
- Add Shading

Tip

The ruler at the top of your screen displays three symbols that let you indent paragraphs in your document.

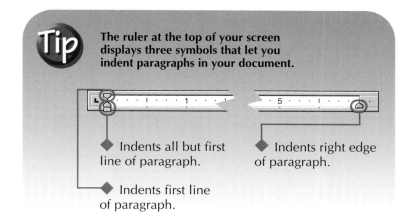

◆ Indents all but first line of paragraph.

◆ Indents right edge of paragraph.

◆ Indents first line of paragraph.

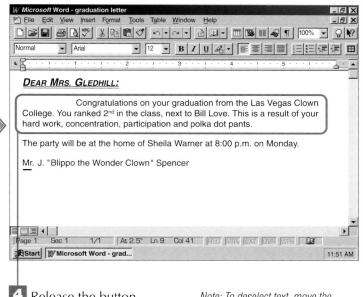

4 Release the button and Word indents the paragraph(s) you selected.

Note: To deselect text, move the mouse I outside the selected area and then press the left button.

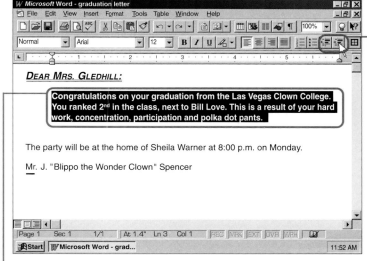

QUICKLY INDENT A PARAGRAPH

1 Select the paragraph(s) you want to indent.

Note: To select text, refer to page 10.

2 Move the mouse ⬧ over one of the following options and then press the left button.

⬚ Moves paragraph(s) right one tab stop.

⬚ Moves paragraph(s) left one tab stop.

> You can enhance the appearance of your document by aligning text in different ways.

Right

Center

Left

Justify

CHANGE PARAGRAPH ALIGNMENT

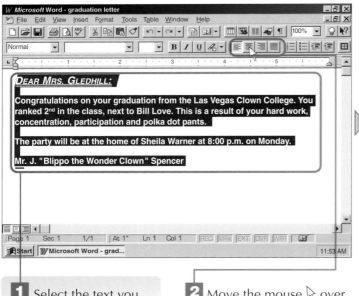

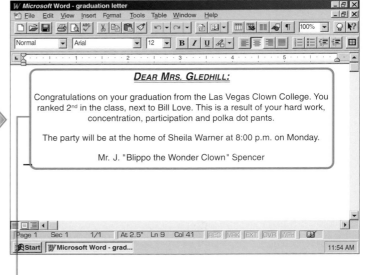

1 Select the text you want to align differently.

Note: To select text, refer to page 10.

2 Move the mouse ▷ over one of the following options and then press the left button.

▤ Left align text

▤ Center text

▤ Right align text

▤ Justify text

◆ The text displays the new alignment.

Note: To deselect text, move the mouse I outside the selected area and then press the left button.

- Change Line Spacing
- Indent a Paragraph
- **Change Paragraph Alignment**
- **Add Bullets or Numbers**
- Change Tab Settings
- Add Borders
- Add Shading

Word can automatically create a numbered or bulleted list as you type.

ADD BULLETS OR NUMBERS

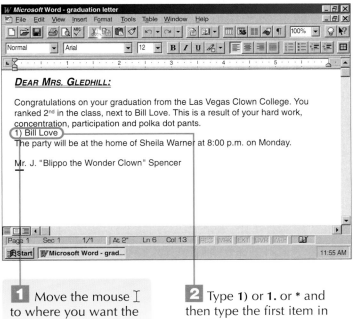

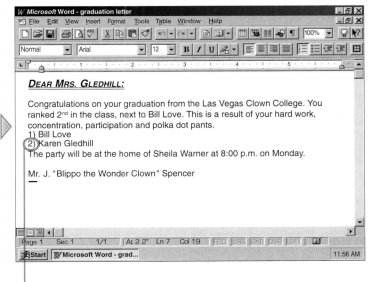

1 Move the mouse I to where you want the first number or bullet to appear and then press the left button.

2 Type **1)** or **1.** or ***** and then type the first item in the list.

3 Press **Enter** on your keyboard and Word automatically starts the next item with a number or bullet.

◆ To end the numbered or bulleted list, press **Enter** on your keyboard twice.

ADD BULLETS OR NUMBERS

You can separate items in a list by beginning each item with a bullet or number.

- Bullets are useful for items in no particular order, such as a list of goals.

Goals for the end of the year:
- Pay off the mortgage
- Save money for a vacation
- Finish painting the house
- Join a health club
- Read more books
- Do volunteer work in the community

Recipe:
1. Preheat oven to 300°F
2. Grate 1 cup of cheese
3. Dice 1/4 cup of onions
4. Slice 1/2 a red pepper into strips
5. Add cheese, onions and red pepper to meat sauce
6. Bake for 20 minutes

- Numbers are useful for items in a specific order, such as a recipe.

ADD BULLETS OR NUMBERS

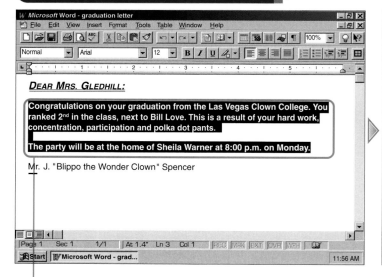

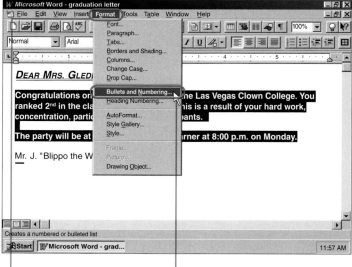

1 Select the paragraphs you want to display bullets or numbers.

Note: To select text, refer to page 10.

2 Move the mouse ⬏ over **Format** and then press the left button.

3 Move the mouse ⬏ over **Bullets and Numbering** and then press the left button.

◆ The **Bullets and Numbering** dialog box appears.

- Change Line Spacing
- Indent a Paragraph
- Change Paragraph Alignment
- **Add Bullets or Numbers**

- Change Tab Settings
- Add Borders
- Add Shading

Tip

You can quickly remove bullets or numbers from a list in your document.

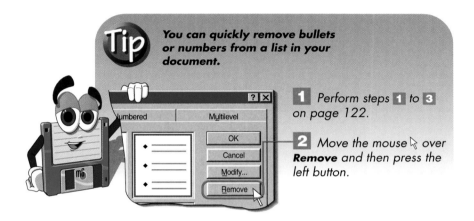

1 Perform steps **1** to **3** on page 122.

2 Move the mouse ⬚ over **Remove** and then press the left button.

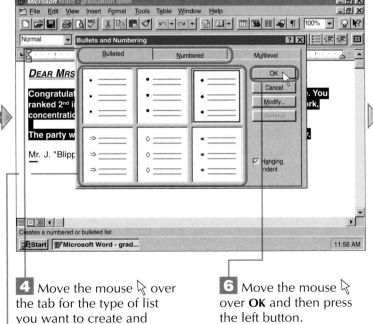

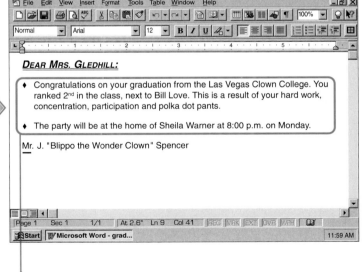

4 Move the mouse ⬚ over the tab for the type of list you want to create and then press the left button.

5 Move the mouse ⬚ over the style you want to use and then press the left button.

6 Move the mouse ⬚ over **OK** and then press the left button.

◆ The bullets or numbers appear in your document.

Note: To deselect text, move the mouse ⌶ outside the selected area and then press the left button.

CHANGE TAB SETTINGS

You can use tab stops to line up columns of information in your document. Word offers four types of tab stops.

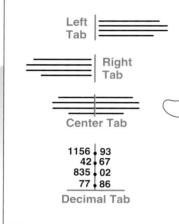

Left Tab

Right Tab

Center Tab

1156	93
42	67
835	02
77	86

Decimal Tab

ADD A TAB STOP

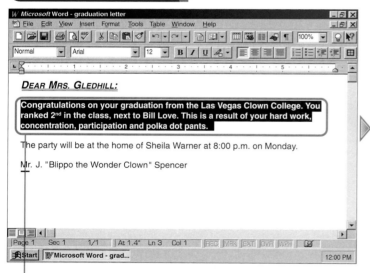

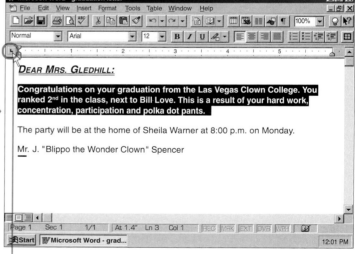

1 Select the text you want to contain the new tab stop.

Note: To select text, refer to page 10.

◆ To add a tab stop to text you are about to type, move the mouse I to where you want the text to appear and then press the left button.

2 Move the mouse ⬚ over this area and then press the left button until the type of tab stop you want to add appears.

Note: If the ruler is not displayed on your screen, refer to page 85 to display the ruler.

⌞ Left tab stop
⊥ Center tab stop
⌟ Right tab stop
⊥ Decimal tab stop

- Change Line Spacing
- Indent a Paragraph
- Change Paragraph Alignment
- Add Bullets or Numbers
- Change Tab Settings
- Add Borders
- Add Shading

Make sure you use tabs rather than spaces to line up columns of text. This will ensure your document prints correctly.

◆ Spaces were used to line up these columns.

◆ Tabs were used to line up these columns.

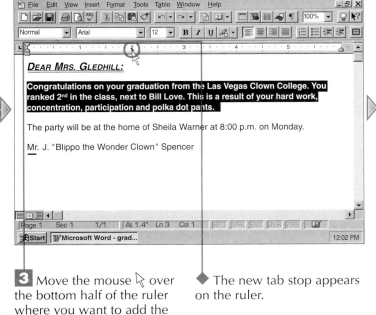

3 Move the mouse ⬦ over the bottom half of the ruler where you want to add the tab stop and then press the left button.

◆ The new tab stop appears on the ruler.

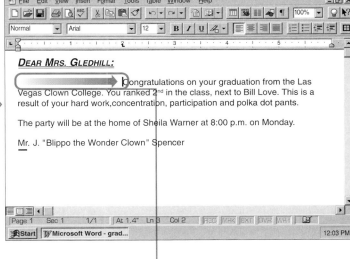

USING TABS

After you have set tabs, you can use them to quickly move the insertion point across your screen.

1 Move the mouse I to the beginning of the line you want to move across and then press the left button.

2 Press **Tab** on your keyboard and the insertion point and all text that follows move to the first tab stop.

CHANGE TAB SETTINGS

> You can have Word insert a line or row of dots before a tab stop to help lead the eye from one column of information to another.

Leader characters make information such as a table of contents or telephone list easier to read.

ADD A TAB STOP WITH LEADER CHARACTERS

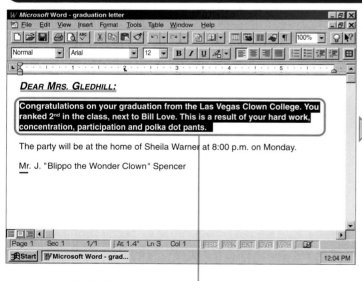

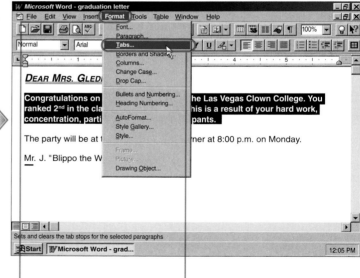

1 Add a tab stop to the text you want to display leader characters.

Note: To add a tab stop, refer to page 124.

2 Select the text containing the tab stop.

Note: To select text, refer to page 10.

3 Move the mouse ⌖ over **Format** and then press the left button.

4 Move the mouse ⌖ over **Tabs** and then press the left button.

◆ The **Tabs** dialog box appears.

- Change Line Spacing
- Indent a Paragraph
- Change Paragraph Alignment
- Add Bullets or Numbers
- **Change Tab Settings**
- Add Borders
- Add Shading

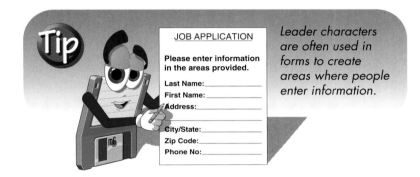

Tip

JOB APPLICATION

Please enter information in the areas provided.

Last Name:_____
First Name:_____
Address:_____

City/State:_____
Zip Code:_____
Phone No:_____

Leader characters are often used in forms to create areas where people enter information.

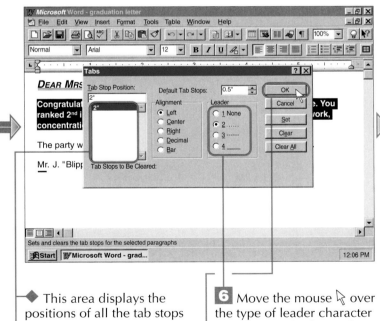

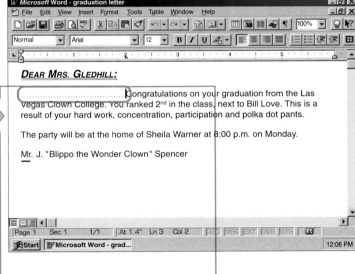

◆ This area displays the positions of all the tab stops you have added to the document.

5 Move the mouse ▷ over the tab stop you want to display leader characters and then press the left button.

6 Move the mouse ▷ over the type of leader character you want to display and then press the left button (○ changes to ◉).

7 Move the mouse ▷ over **OK** and then press the left button.

USING TABS

After you have set tabs, you can use them to quickly move the insertion point across your screen.

1 Move the mouse I to the beginning of the line you want to move across and then press the left button.

2 Press **Tab** on your keyboard and the insertion point and all text that follows move to the first tab stop.

◆ Word places a line or row of dots before the insertion point.

127

CHANGE TAB SETTINGS

You can easily move a tab stop to a different position on the ruler.

MOVE A TAB STOP

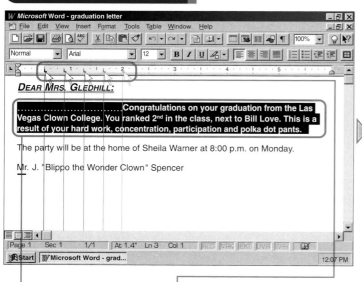

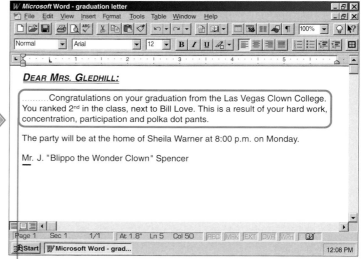

1 Select the text containing the tab stop you want to move.

Note: To select text, refer to page 10.

2 Move the mouse ⌖ over the tab stop and then press and hold down the left button as you drag the tab stop to a new position.

◆ A line shows the new position.

3 Release the button and the text containing the tab stop moves to the new position.

Note: To deselect text, move the mouse ⌶ outside the selected area and then press the left button.

- Change Line Spacing
- Indent a Paragraph
- Change Paragraph Alignment
- Add Bullets or Numbers
- **Change Tab Settings**
- Add Borders
- Add Shading

When you no longer need a tab stop, you can remove it from the ruler.

REMOVE A TAB STOP

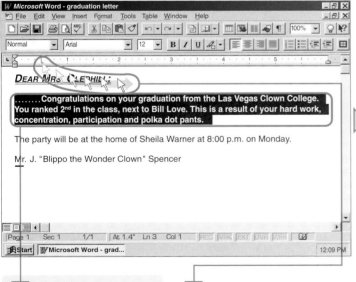

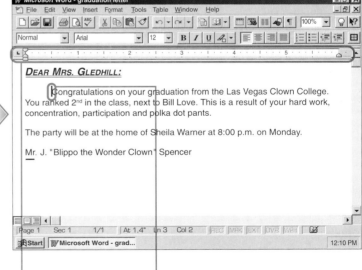

1 Select the text containing the tab stop you want to remove.

Note: To select text, refer to page 10.

2 Move the mouse � over the tab stop and then press and hold down the left button as you drag the tab stop downward off the ruler.

3 Release the button and the tab stop disappears from the ruler.

◆ To move the text back to the left margin, move the mouse I to the left of the first character in the paragraph and then press the left button. Then press ⬅Backspace on your keyboard.

ADD BORDERS

You can add borders to emphasize a section of text in your document.

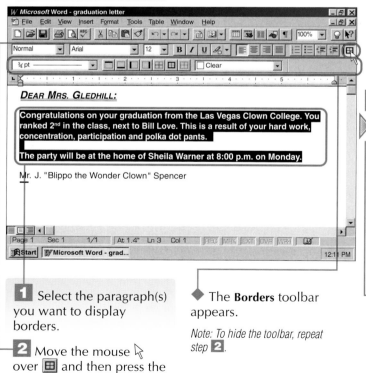

1 Select the paragraph(s) you want to display borders.

2 Move the mouse ⌖ over ▦ and then press the left button.

◆ The **Borders** toolbar appears.

Note: To hide the toolbar, repeat step 2.

3 To display a list of the available line styles, move the mouse ⌖ over this area and then press the left button.

4 Move the mouse ⌖ over the line style you want to use and then press the left button.

Note: To view all the available line styles, use the scroll bar. For more information, refer to page 13.

- Change Line Spacing
- Indent a Paragraph
- Change Paragraph Alignment
- Add Bullets or Numbers
- Change Tab Settings
- **Add Borders**
- Add Shading

Tip

You can quickly add a line to your document.

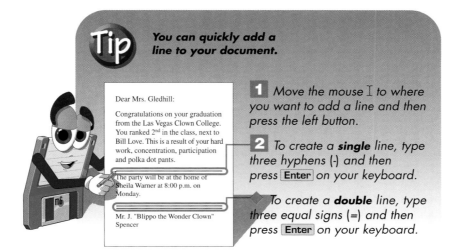

1 Move the mouse I to where you want to add a line and then press the left button.

2 To create a **single** line, type three hyphens (-) and then press **Enter** on your keyboard.

To create a **double** line, type three equal signs (=) and then press **Enter** on your keyboard.

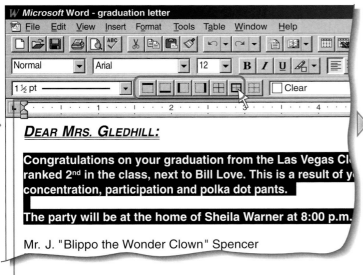

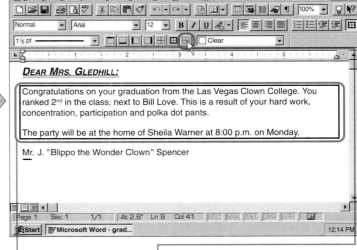

5 Move the mouse ⤸ over one of the border options and then press the left button.

◻ ◻ ◻ ◻ Edges of paragraphs

▦ Between paragraphs

▣ Around paragraphs

6 Repeat steps **3** to **5** for each border you want to add.

◆ The borders you selected appear.

Note: To deselect text, move the mouse I outside the selected area and then press the left button.

REMOVE BORDERS

1 Select the paragraph(s) you no longer want to display borders.

2 Move the mouse ⤸ over ▦ on the **Borders** toolbar and then press the left button.

ADD SHADING

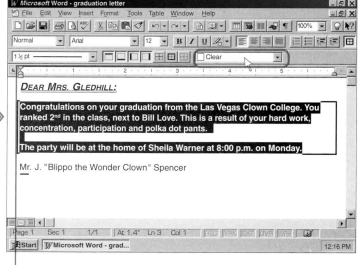

You can improve the appearance of your document by adding shading.

ADD SHADING

1 Select the paragraph(s) you want to display shading.

2 Move the mouse ⏸ over 田 and then press the left button.

◆ The **Borders** toolbar appears.

*Note: To hide the toolbar, repeat step **2**.*

3 To display a list of the available shading options, move the mouse ⏸ over this area and then press the left button.

- Change Line Spacing
- Indent a Paragraph
- Change Paragraph Alignment
- Add Bullets or Numbers
- Change Tab Settings
- Add Borders
- **Add Shading**

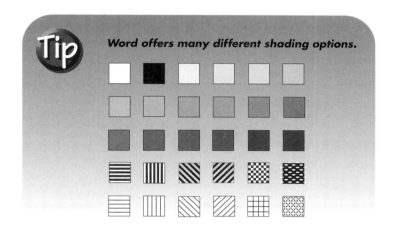

Tip

Word offers many different shading options.

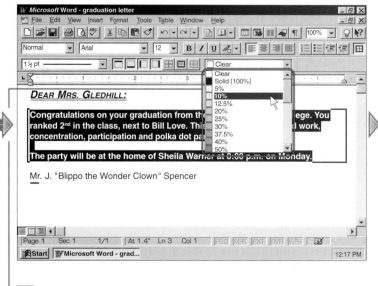

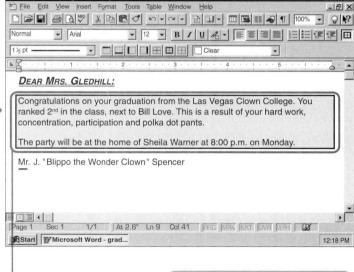

4 Move the mouse ⍓ over the shading option you want to use and then press the left button.

Note: To view all the available options, use the scroll bar. For more information, refer to page 13.

◆ The shading you selected appears.

Note: To deselect a paragraph, move the mouse Ⲓ outside the selected area and then press the left button.

REMOVE SHADING

1 Select the paragraph(s) you no longer want to display shading.

2 Perform steps **3** and **4**, selecting **Clear** in step **4**.

133

FORMAT PAGES

ADD PAGE NUMBERS

You can have Word number the pages in your document.

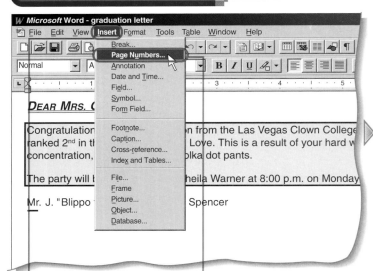

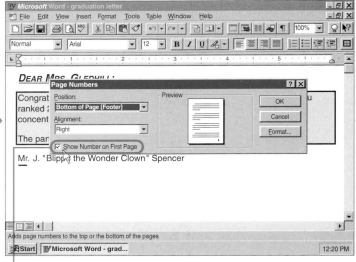

1 Move the mouse ▷ over **Insert** and then press the left button.

2 Move the mouse ▷ over **Page Numbers** and then press the left button.

◆ The **Page Numbers** dialog box appears.

3 To hide the page number on the first page of your document, move the mouse ▷ over this option and then press the left button (☑ changes to ☐).

Note: This option is useful if the first page of your document is a title page.

- **Add Page Numbers**
- Add Footnotes
- Add a Header or Footer
- Edit a Header or Footer

- Format a Document Automatically
- Insert a Page Break
- Create a New Section
- Center a Page

- Change Margins
- Change Paper Size
- Change Page Orientation
- Create Columns

Tip

You can use the Print Preview feature to display page numbers on your screen. This lets you see how the page numbers will look before you print the document.

Note: For information on using Print Preview, refer to pages 68 to 71.

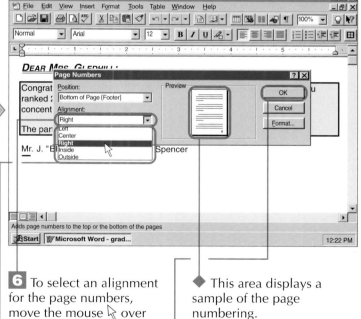

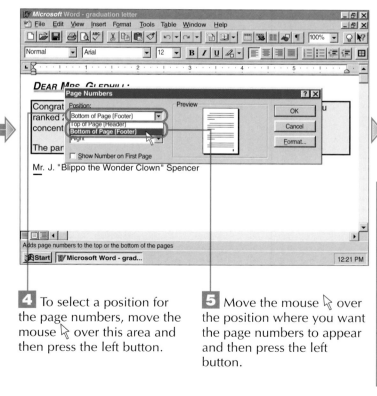

4 To select a position for the page numbers, move the mouse ⟍ over this area and then press the left button.

5 Move the mouse ⟍ over the position where you want the page numbers to appear and then press the left button.

6 To select an alignment for the page numbers, move the mouse ⟍ over this area and then press the left button.

7 Move the mouse ⟍ over the alignment you want to use and then press the left button.

◆ This area displays a sample of the page numbering.

8 Move the mouse ⟍ over **OK** and then press the left button.

ADD FOOTNOTES

A footnote appears at the bottom of a page to provide additional information about text in your document.

Word automatically numbers a footnote and places the footnote on the same page as the text it refers to.

1 H. Smith, _Aeronautical Refrigeration Repair_ (California: Quest Publishing, 1989) 10.

2 R. Anderson, _Volatile Cold Gases_ (Alaska: Inert Publishing, 1992) 31.

ADD FOOTNOTES

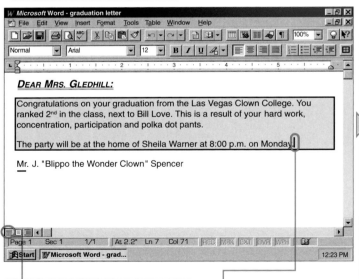

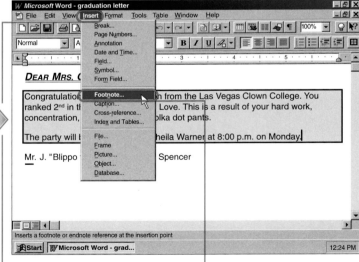

1 To display your document in the normal view, move the mouse ⤐ over ▤ and then press the left button.

2 Move the mouse I to where you want the number of the footnote to appear and then press the left button.

3 Move the mouse ⤐ over **Insert** and then press the left button.

4 Move the mouse ⤐ over **Footnote** and then press the left button.

- Add Page Numbers
- **Add Footnotes**
- Add a Header or Footer
- Edit a Header or Footer

- Format a Document Automatically
- Insert a Page Break
- Create a New Section
- Center a Page

- Change Margins
- Change Paper Size
- Change Page Orientation
- Create Columns

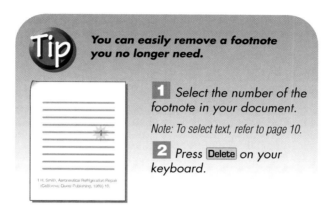

Tip

You can easily remove a footnote you no longer need.

1 Select the number of the footnote in your document.

Note: To select text, refer to page 10.

2 Press Delete on your keyboard.

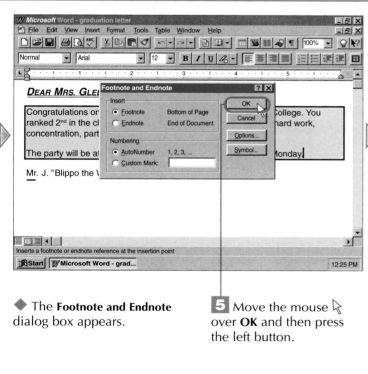

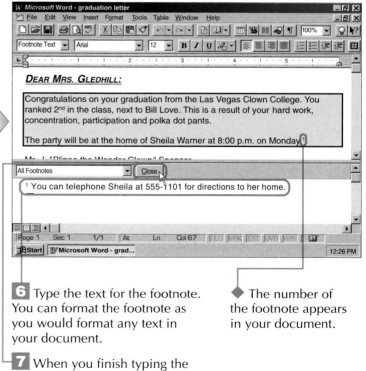

◆ The **Footnote and Endnote** dialog box appears.

5 Move the mouse over **OK** and then press the left button.

6 Type the text for the footnote. You can format the footnote as you would format any text in your document.

7 When you finish typing the footnote, move the mouse over **Close** and then press the left button.

◆ The number of the footnote appears in your document.

139

ADD A HEADER OR FOOTER

You can add a header or footer to each page of your document to display information such as the date or your company name.

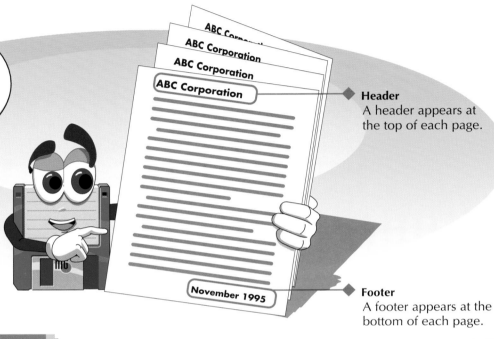

Header
A header appears at the top of each page.

Footer
A footer appears at the bottom of each page.

ADD A HEADER OR FOOTER

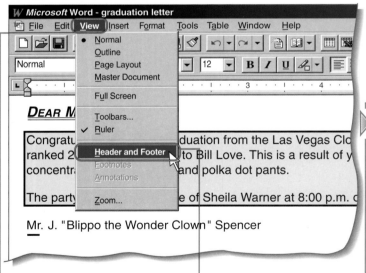

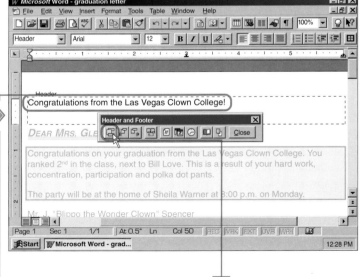

1 Move the mouse over **View** and then press the left button.

2 Move the mouse over **Header and Footer** and then press the left button.

◆ The text in your document is dimmed.

3 To create a header, type the header text. You can format the text as you would format any text in your document.

4 To create a footer, move the mouse over ▣ and then press the left button.

- Add Page Numbers
- Add Footnotes
- Add a Header or Footer
- Edit a Header or Footer

- Format a Document Automatically
- Insert a Page Break
- Create a New Section
- Center a Page

- Change Margins
- Change Paper Size
- Change Page Orientation
- Create Columns

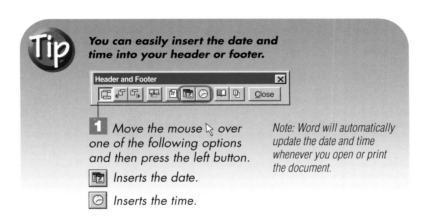

Tip

You can easily insert the date and time into your header or footer.

1 Move the mouse ⟨ over one of the following options and then press the left button.

Inserts the date.

Inserts the time.

Note: Word will automatically update the date and time whenever you open or print the document.

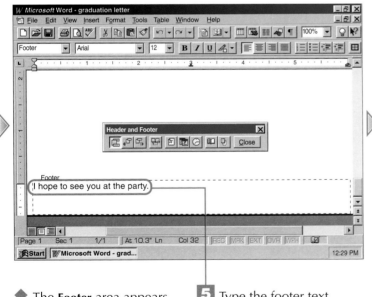

◆ The **Footer** area appears.

Note: To return to the header area at any time, repeat step **4**.

5 Type the footer text. You can format the text as you would format any text in your document.

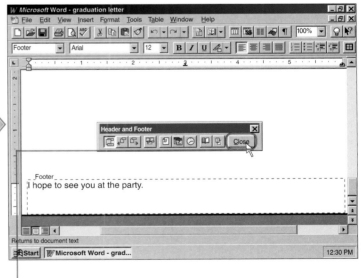

6 When you have finished creating the header or footer, move the mouse ⟨ over **Close** and then press the left button.

Note: To edit header or footer text, refer to page 142.

EDIT A HEADER OR FOOTER

FORMAT A DOCUMENT AUTOMATICALLY

> You can easily change a header or footer. Word will automatically change the header or footer on every page in your document.

EDIT A HEADER OR FOOTER

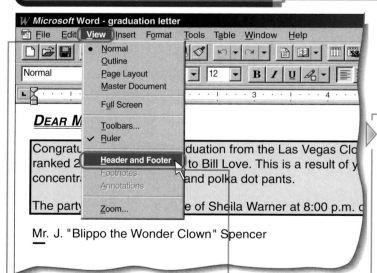

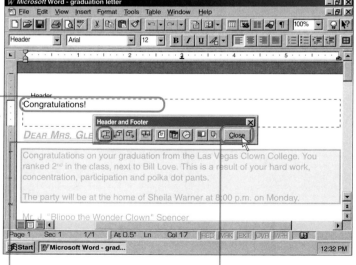

1 To display the header or footer you want to edit, move the mouse ↕ over **View** and then press the left button.

2 Move the mouse ↕ over **Header and Footer** and then press the left button.

◆ To switch between the header and footer areas, move the mouse ↕ over 🔁 and then press the left button.

3 Edit the header or footer as you would edit any text in your document.

4 When you have finished editing the header or footer, move the mouse ↕ over **Close** and then press the left button.

142

- Add Page Numbers
- Add Footnotes
- Add a Header or Footer
- **Edit a Header or Footer**

- **Format a Document Automatically**
- Insert a Page Break
- Create a New Section
- Center a Page

- Change Margins
- Change Paper Size
- Change Page Orientation
- Create Columns

You can have Word choose the design that best suits your document and then apply the design for you.

FORMAT A DOCUMENT AUTOMATICALLY

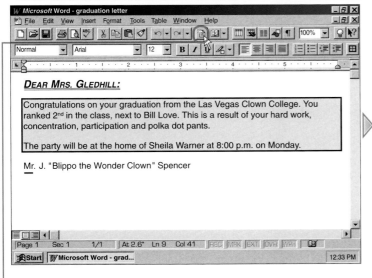

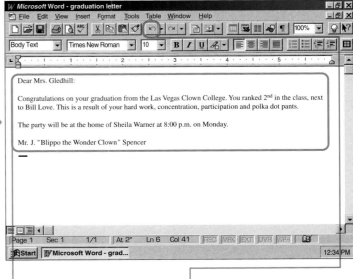

1 Move the mouse over 📄 and then press the left button.

◆ The document displays the new design.

◆ If you do not like the new design, immediately move the mouse over ↺ and then press the left button.

143

INSERT A PAGE BREAK

> If you want to start a new page at a specific place in your document, you can insert a page break. A page break shows where one page ends and another begins.

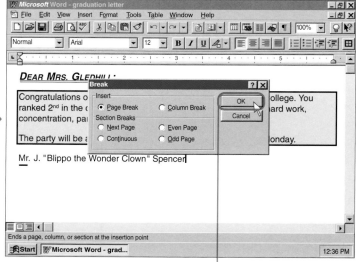

INSERT A PAGE BREAK

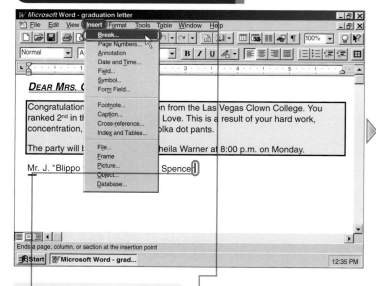

1 Move the mouse I to where you want to start a new page and then press the left button.

2 Move the mouse ▷ over **Insert** and then press the left button.

3 Move the mouse ▷ over **Break** and then press the left button.

◆ The **Break** dialog box appears.

4 Move the mouse ▷ over **OK** and then press the left button.

- Add Page Numbers
- Add Footnotes
- Add a Header or Footer
- Edit a Header or Footer
- Format a Document Automatically
- **Insert a Page Break**
- Create a New Section
- Center a Page
- Change Margins
- Change Paper Size
- Change Page Orientation
- Create Columns

Tip

When you fill a page with text, Word automatically starts a new one by inserting a page break for you.

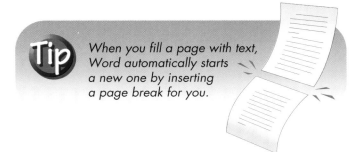

REMOVE A PAGE BREAK

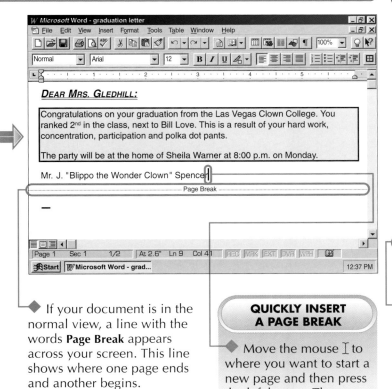

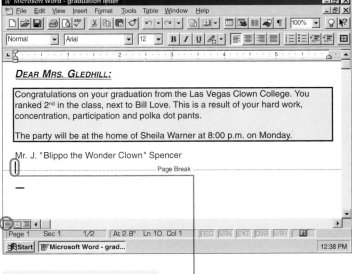

◆ If your document is in the normal view, a line with the words **Page Break** appears across your screen. This line shows where one page ends and another begins.

Note: This line will not appear when you print your document.

QUICKLY INSERT A PAGE BREAK

◆ Move the mouse I to where you want to start a new page and then press the left button. Then press Ctrl + Enter on your keyboard.

1 To display your document in the normal view, move the mouse over the button and then press the left button.

2 Move the mouse I over the **Page Break** line and then press the left button.

3 Press Delete on your keyboard.

CREATE A NEW SECTION

If you want parts of your document to look different, you must divide the document into sections. This lets you format each section separately.

Section 1

Section 2

Section 3

CREATE A NEW SECTION

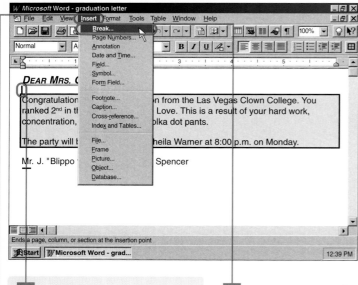

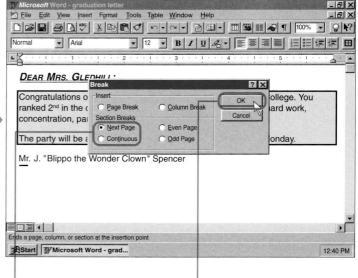

1 Move the mouse I to where you want to start a new section and then press the left button.

2 Move the mouse ♱ over **Insert** and then press the left button.

3 Move the mouse ♱ over **Break** and then press the left button.

◆ The **Break** dialog box appears.

4 Move the mouse ♱ over the type of section break you want to create and then press the left button.

Next Page - Creates a new section on a new page.

Continuous - Creates a new section on the current page.

5 Move the mouse ♱ over **OK** and then press the left button.

146

- Add Page Numbers
- Add Footnotes
- Add a Header or Footer
- Edit a Header or Footer
- Format a Document Automatically
- Insert a Page Break
- **Create a New Section**
- Center a Page
- Change Margins
- Change Paper Size
- Change Page Orientation
- Create Columns

When you remove a section break, the text above the break assumes the appearance of the following section.

REMOVE A SECTION BREAK

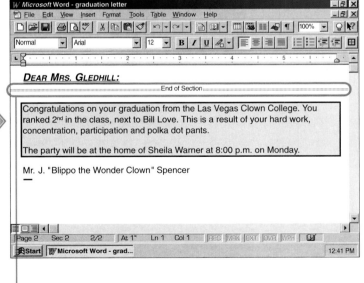

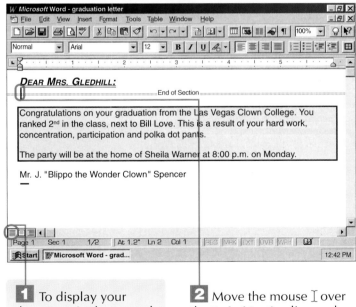

◆ If your document is in the normal view, a line with the words **End of Section** appears across your screen. This line shows where one section ends and another begins.

Note: This line will not appear when you print your document.

1 To display your document in the normal view, move the mouse over ▤ and then press the left button.

2 Move the mouse I over the **End of Section** line and then press the left button.

3 Press **Delete** on your keyboard.

You can vertically center text on a page. This is useful for creating title pages or short memos.

CENTER A PAGE

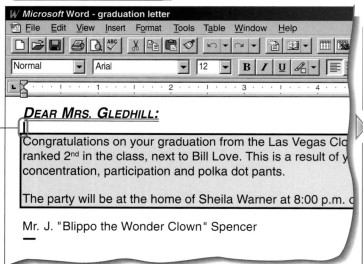

1 Move the mouse I anywhere over the document or section you want to vertically center and then press the left button.

Note: To center only a part of your document, you must first divide the document into sections. For more information, refer to page 146.

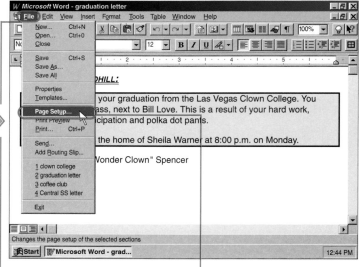

2 Move the mouse ⤢ over **File** and then press the left button.

3 Move the mouse ⤢ over **Page Setup** and then press the left button.

◆ The **Page Setup** dialog box appears.

- Add Page Numbers
- Add Footnotes
- Add a Header or Footer
- Edit a Header or Footer

- Format a Document Automatically
- Insert a Page Break
- Create a New Section
- **Center a Page**

- Change Margins
- Change Paper Size
- Change Page Orientation
- Create Columns

Tip

You can use the Print Preview feature to display the centered page on your screen. This lets you see how the page will look before you print the document.

Note: For information on using Print Preview, refer to pages 68 to 71.

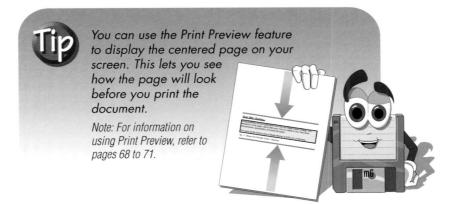

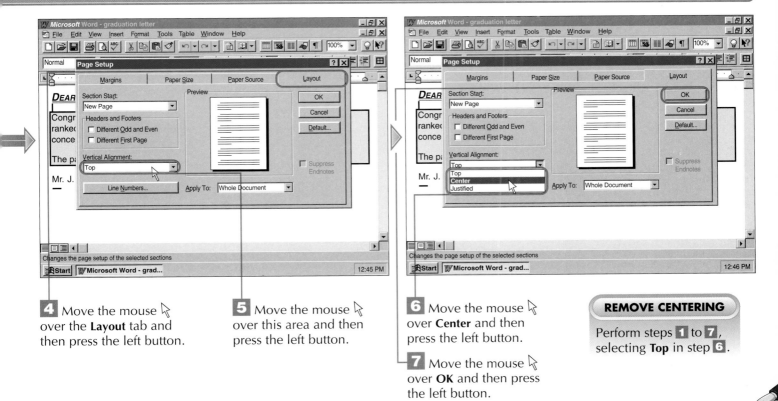

4 Move the mouse ⇱ over the **Layout** tab and then press the left button.

5 Move the mouse ⇱ over this area and then press the left button.

6 Move the mouse ⇱ over **Center** and then press the left button.

7 Move the mouse ⇱ over **OK** and then press the left button.

REMOVE CENTERING

Perform steps **1** to **7**, selecting **Top** in step **6**.

CHANGE MARGINS

A margin is the amount of space between text and an edge of your paper. You can easily change the margins to suit your document.

Changing margins lets you change the length of your document or accommodate letterhead and other specialty paper.

CHANGE MARGINS

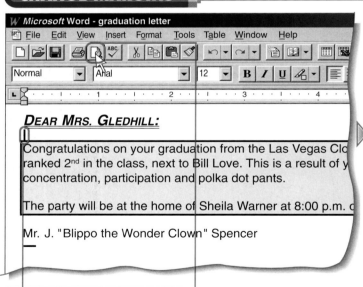

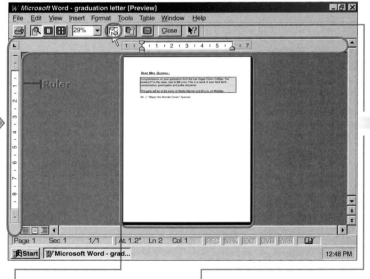

1 Move the mouse I anywhere over the document or section where you want to change the margins and then press the left button.

Note: To change the margins for only a part of your document, you must first divide the document into sections. For more information, refer to page 146.

2 Move the mouse ⌖ over 🔲 and then press the left button.

◆ Your document appears in the Print Preview window.

Note: For more information on using Print Preview, refer to pages 68 to 71.

3 To display the ruler, move the mouse ⌖ over 🔲 and then press the left button.

- Add Page Numbers
- Add Footnotes
- Add a Header or Footer
- Edit a Header or Footer

- Format a Document Automatically
- Insert a Page Break
- Create a New Section
- Center a Page

- **Change Margins**
- Change Paper Size
- Change Page Orientation
- Create Columns

Tip

If you want to change the left and right margins for a part of your document, it is much easier to change the indentation.

Note: For information on indenting paragraphs, refer to page 118.

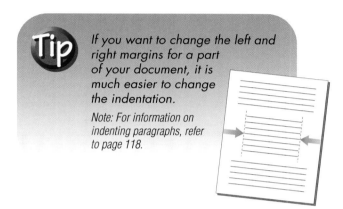

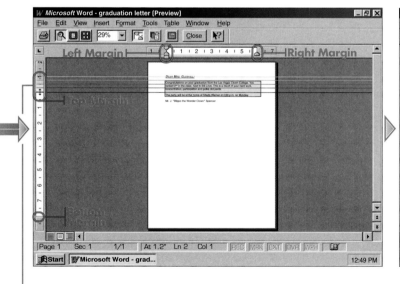

4 Move the mouse ⬉ over the margin you want to move (⬉ changes to ↕ or ↔) and then press and hold down the left button as you drag the margin to a new location.

◆ A line shows the new location.

5 Release the button and the margin moves to the new location.

6 Repeat steps **4** and **5** for each margin you want to move.

7 To close the Print Preview window, move the mouse ⬉ over **Close** and then press the left button.

Word automatically sets each page in your document to print on 8.5 by 11 inch paper. If you want to use a different paper size, you can change this setting.

CHANGE PAPER SIZE

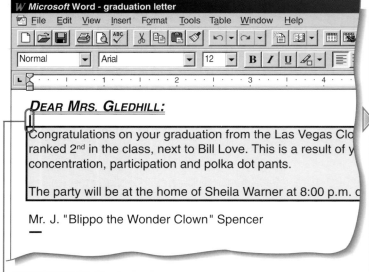

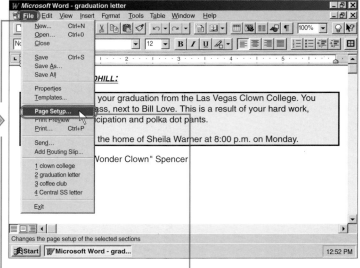

1 Move the mouse I anywhere over the document or section you want to print on a new paper size and then press the left button.

Note: To change the paper size for only a part of your document, you must first divide the document into sections. For more information, refer to page 146.

2 Move the mouse ▹ over **File** and then press the left button.

3 Move the mouse ▹ over **Page Setup** and then press the left button.

◆ The **Page Setup** dialog box appears.

- Add Page Numbers
- Add Footnotes
- Add a Header or Footer
- Edit a Header or Footer

- Format a Document Automatically
- Insert a Page Break
- Create a New Section
- Center a Page

- Change Margins
- **Change Paper Size**
- Change Page Orientation
- Create Columns

Tip

*The available paper sizes listed in the **Page Setup** dialog box depend on the printer you are using.*

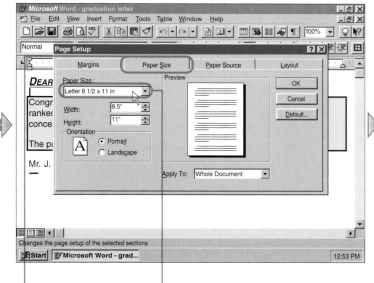

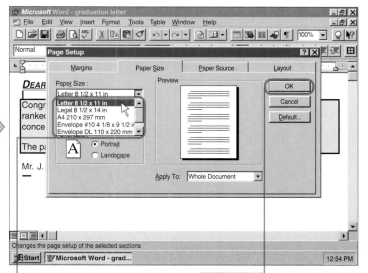

4 Move the mouse ⅓ over the **Paper Size** tab and then press the left button.

◆ This area displays the current paper size.

5 To display a list of the available paper sizes for your printer, move the mouse ⅓ over this area and then press the left button.

6 Move the mouse ⅓ over the paper size you want to use and then press the left button.

7 Move the mouse ⅓ over **OK** and then press the left button.

CHANGE PAGE ORIENTATION

You can change the orientation of text on a page.

Portrait   Landscape

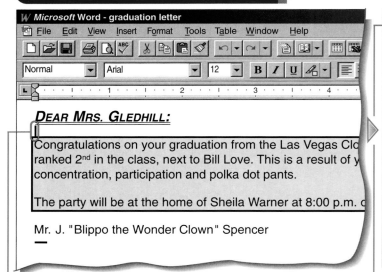

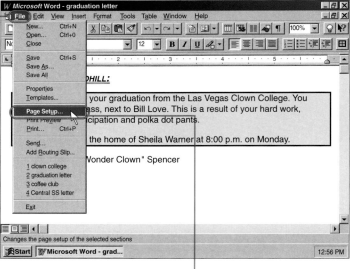

1 Move the mouse I anywhere over the document or section you want to print in a different orientation and then press the left button.

Note: To change the orientation for only a part of your document, you must first divide the document into sections. For more information, refer to page 146.

2 Move the mouse ⊳ over **File** and then press the left button.

3 Move the mouse ⊳ over **Page Setup** and then press the left button.

◆ The **Page Setup** dialog box appears.

- Add Page Numbers
- Add Footnotes
- Add a Header or Footer
- Edit a Header or Footer

- Format a Document Automatically
- Insert a Page Break
- Create a New Section
- Center a Page

- Change Margins
- Change Paper Size
- **Change Page Orientation**
- Create Columns

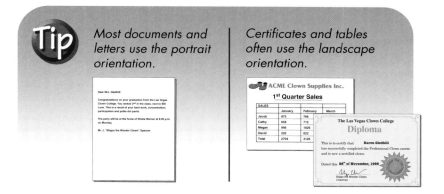

Tip

Most documents and letters use the portrait orientation.

Certificates and tables often use the landscape orientation.

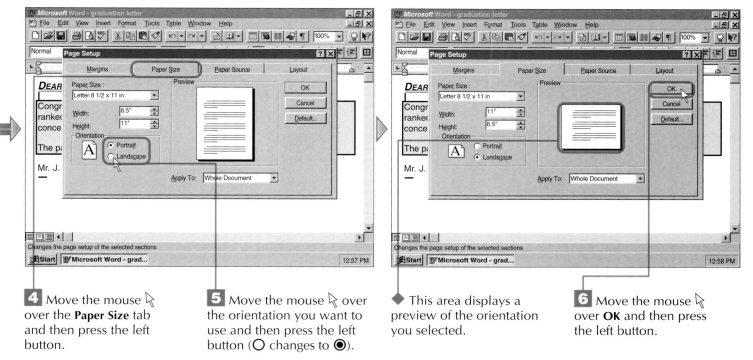

4 Move the mouse ⬡ over the **Paper Size** tab and then press the left button.

5 Move the mouse ⬡ over the orientation you want to use and then press the left button (○ changes to ⦿).

◆ This area displays a preview of the orientation you selected.

6 Move the mouse ⬡ over **OK** and then press the left button.

155

CREATE COLUMNS

You can display your text in columns like those found in a newspaper. This is useful for creating documents such as newsletters and brochures.

CREATE COLUMNS

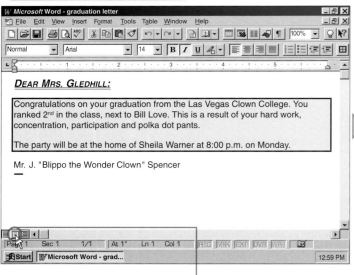

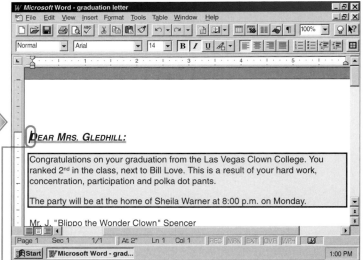

◆ Word cannot display columns side-by-side in the normal view.

1 To display your document in the page layout view, move the mouse ▷ over ▤ and then press the left button.

◆ Your document appears in the page layout view.

2 Move the mouse I anywhere over the document or section you want to display in columns and then press the left button.

Note: To create columns for only a part of your document, you must first divide the document into sections. For more information, refer to page 146.

- Add Page Numbers
- Add Footnotes
- Add a Header or Footer
- Edit a Header or Footer

- Format a Document Automatically
- Insert a Page Break
- Create a New Section
- Center a Page

- Change Margins
- Change Paper Size
- Change Page Orientation
- **Create Columns**

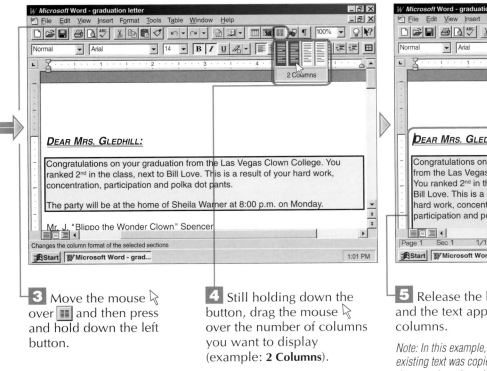

Word lets you quickly create up to six columns in your document.

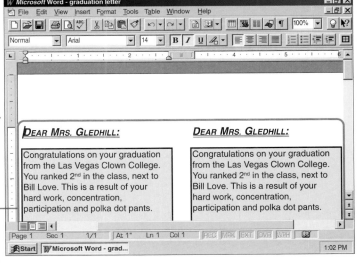

3 Move the mouse over ▤ and then press and hold down the left button.

4 Still holding down the button, drag the mouse over the number of columns you want to display (example: **2 Columns**).

5 Release the button and the text appears in columns.

Note: In this example, the existing text was copied three times to show the columns. To copy text, refer to page 46.

REMOVE COLUMNS

Repeat steps **1** to **5**, selecting **1 Column** in step **4**.

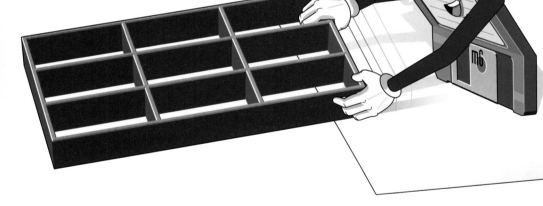

WORKING WITH TABLES

- Create a Table
- Add a Row or Column
- Delete a Row or Column
- Delete a Table
- Change Column Width
- Merge Cells
- Add Borders to a Table
- Format a Table

SALES	January	February	March
Jason	875	726	845
Allan	658	589	697
Cathy	946	963	831
Lawrence	876	649	954

You can create a table to help organize information.

CREATE A TABLE

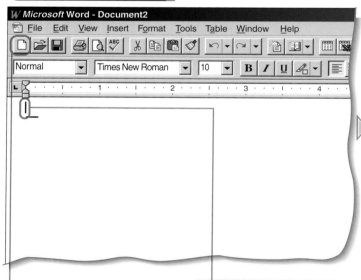

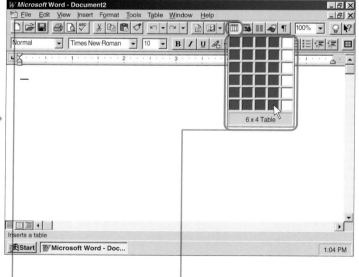

◆ In this example, a new document was created. To create a new document, move the mouse ↳ over 🗋 and then press the left button.

1 Move the mouse I to where you want the table to appear in your document and then press the left button.

2 Move the mouse ↳ over 🔲 and then press and hold down the left button.

3 Still holding down the button, drag the mouse ↳ over the number of rows and columns you want the table to contain (example: **6 x 4**).

- **Create a Table**
- Add a Row or Column
- Delete a Row or Column
- Delete a Table
- Change Column Width
- Merge Cells
- Add Borders to a Table
- Format a Table

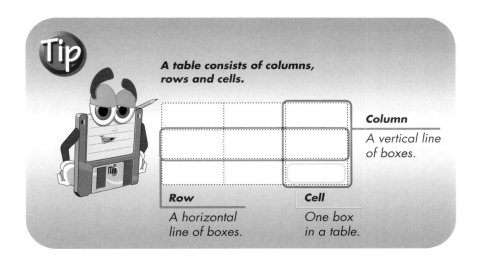

Tip

A table consists of columns, rows and cells.

Column
A vertical line of boxes.

Row
A horizontal line of boxes.

Cell
One box in a table.

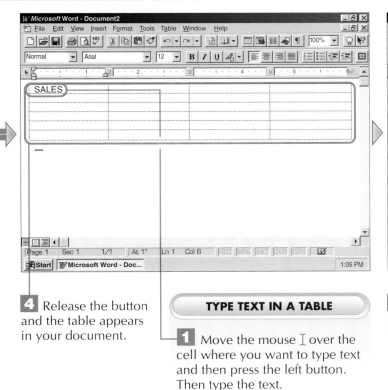

4 Release the button and the table appears in your document.

TYPE TEXT IN A TABLE

1 Move the mouse I over the cell where you want to type text and then press the left button. Then type the text.

Note: In this example, the design and size of text were changed to make the text easier to read. To change the design and size of text, refer to page 104.

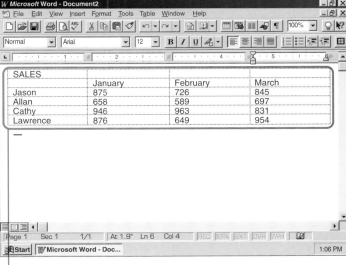

2 Repeat step **1** until you have typed all the text.

◆ You can also use one of the following keys on your keyboard to quickly move through cells in a table.

⬇ Move down one cell.

Tab Move right one cell.

ADD A ROW OR COLUMN

You can add a row or column to your table if you want to insert additional information.

ADD A ROW

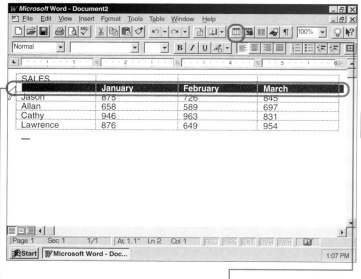

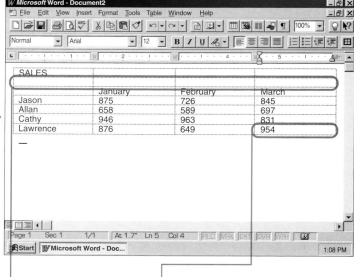

Word will insert a row above the row you select.

1 To select a row, move the mouse I to the left edge of the row (I changes to ↗) and then press the left button.

2 Move the mouse ↖ over 🔲 and then press the left button.

◆ A new row appears.

Note: To deselect a row, move the mouse I outside the selected area and then press the left button.

You can add a row to the bottom of a table.

1 Move the mouse I over the bottom right cell in the table and then press the left button.

2 Press **Tab** on your keyboard.

- Create a Table
- **Add a Row or Column**
- Delete a Row or Column
- Delete a Table

- Change Column Width
- Merge Cells
- Add Borders to a Table
- Format a Table

Tip

You can add a column to the end of a table.

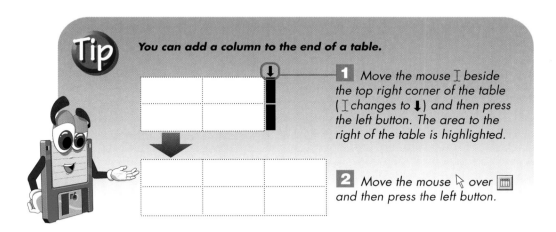

1 Move the mouse I beside the top right corner of the table (I changes to ↓) and then press the left button. The area to the right of the table is highlighted.

2 Move the mouse ☒ over 🖩 and then press the left button.

ADD A COLUMN

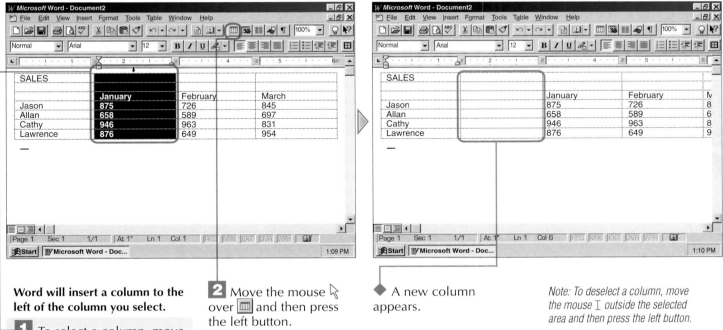

Word will insert a column to the left of the column you select.

1 To select a column, move the mouse I to the top of the column (I changes to ↓) and then press the left button.

2 Move the mouse ☒ over 🖩 and then press the left button.

◆ A new column appears.

Note: To deselect a column, move the mouse I outside the selected area and then press the left button.

163

DELETE A ROW OR COLUMN

You can delete a row or column you no longer need.

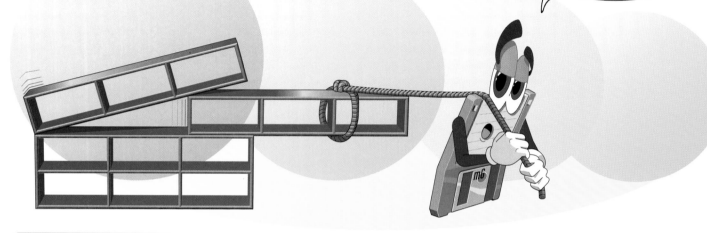

DELETE A ROW

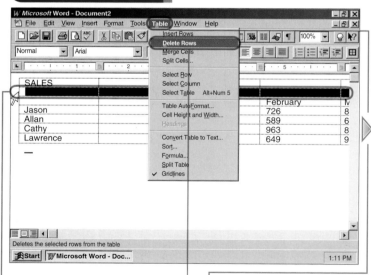

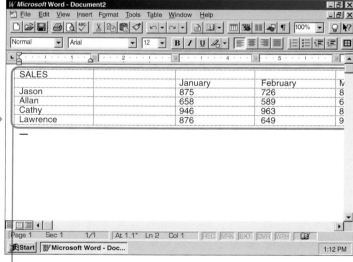

1 To select the row you want to delete, move the mouse I to the left edge of the row (I changes to ⟋) and then press the left button.

2 Move the mouse ⟋ over **Table** and then press the left button.

3 Move the mouse ⟋ over **Delete Rows** and then press the left button.

◆ The row disappears.

- Create a Table
- Add a Row or Column
- **Delete a Row or Column**
- Delete a Table

- Change Column Width
- Merge Cells
- Add Borders to a Table
- Format a Table

Tip

You can easily delete text from your table.

Select the text you want to remove and then press Delete *on your keyboard.*

Note: To select text, refer to page 10.

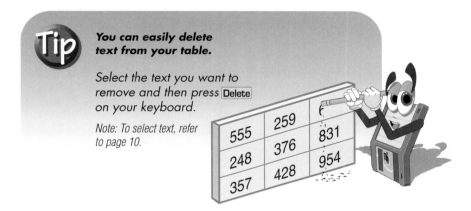

DELETE A COLUMN

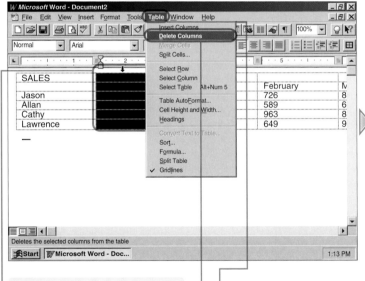

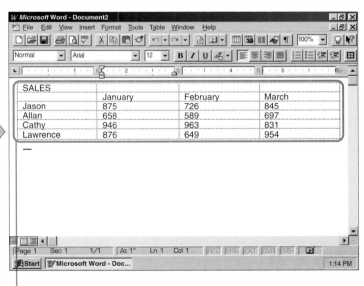

1 To select the column you want to delete, move the mouse I to the top edge of the column (I changes to ↓) and then press the left button.

2 Move the mouse ↘ over **Table** and then press the left button.

3 Move the mouse ↘ over **Delete Columns** and then press the left button.

◆ The column disappears.

165

You can quickly remove an entire table from your document.

DELETE A TABLE

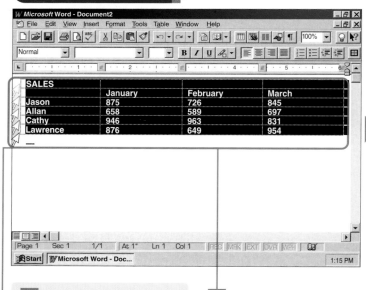

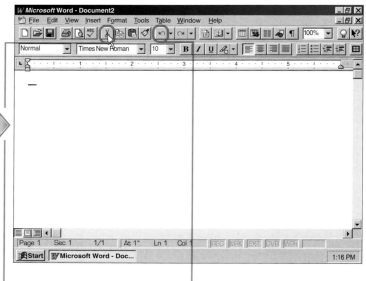

1 To select all the rows in the table you want to delete, move the mouse I to the left of the first row in the table (I changes to ↗).

2 Press and hold down the left button as you drag the mouse ↗ downward until you highlight all the rows. Then release the button.

3 Move the mouse ↗ over ✂ and then press the left button.

◆ The table disappears.

◆ To return the table to your document, immediately move the mouse ↗ over ↺ and then press the left button.

- Create a Table
- Add a Row or Column
- Delete a Row or Column
- **Delete a Table**

- **Change Column Width**
- Merge Cells
- Add Borders to a Table
- Format a Table

You can improve the appearance of your table by changing the width of columns.

CHANGE COLUMN WIDTH

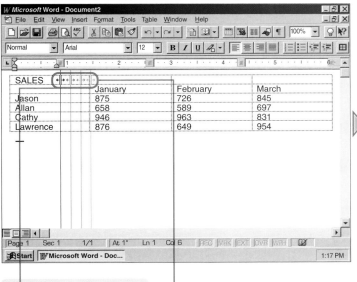

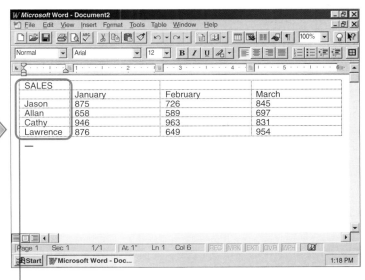

1 Move the mouse I over the column edge you want to move (I changes to ↔).

2 Press and hold down the left button as you drag the column edge to a new position.

◆ A line shows the new position.

3 Release the button and the column displays the new width.

You can have Word change a column width to fit the longest item in the column.

Move the mouse I over the right edge of the column you want to change (I changes to ↔). Then quickly press the left button twice.

167

You can combine two or more cells in your table into one large cell. This is useful if you want to display a title across the top of your table.

MERGE CELLS

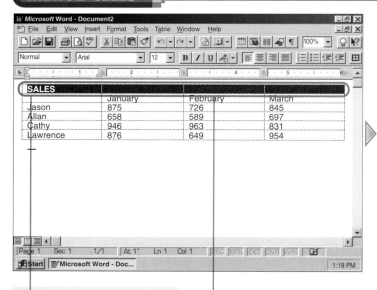

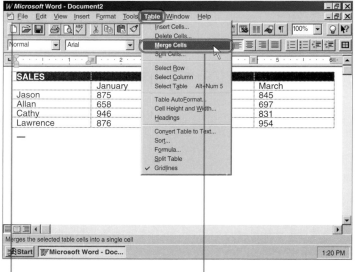

1 To select the cells you want to merge, move the mouse I over the first cell you want to join with other cells.

2 Press and hold down the left button as you drag the mouse I until you highlight all the cells you want to merge.

Note: You can only merge cells in a row. You cannot merge cells in a column.

3 Move the mouse ⌖ over **Table** and then press the left button.

4 Move the mouse ⌖ over **Merge Cells** and then press the left button.

- Create a Table
- Add a Row or Column
- Delete a Row or Column
- Delete a Table
- Change Column Width
- **Merge Cells**
- Add Borders to a Table
- Format a Table

> You can split one cell in your table into several smaller cells.

SPLIT CELLS

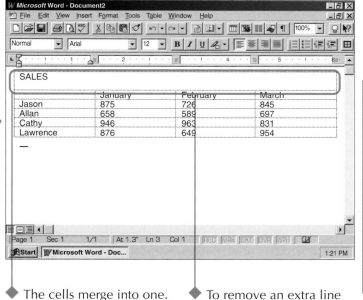

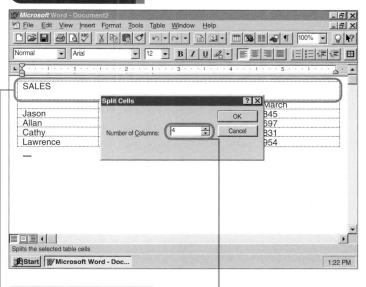

◆ The cells merge into one.

Note: To deselect cells, move the mouse I outside the selected area and then press the left button.

◆ To remove an extra line from the cell, move the mouse I to the right of the last character in the cell and then press the left button. Then press **Delete** on your keyboard.

1 Move the mouse I over the cell you want to split and then press the left button.

2 To display the **Split Cells** dialog box, perform steps **3** and **4** on page 168, selecting **Split Cells** in step **4**.

3 Type the number of columns you want to create (example: **4**) and then press **Enter** on your keyboard.

Note: You can only split a cell into columns. You cannot split a cell into rows.

ADD BORDERS TO A TABLE

You can enhance the appearance of your table by adding borders.

ADD BORDERS TO A TABLE

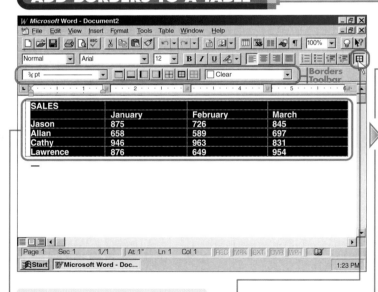

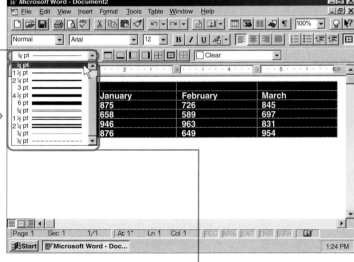

1 To select the cells you want to display borders, move the mouse I over the first cell you want to display a border.

2 Press and hold down the left button as you drag the mouse I until you highlight all the cells you want to display borders.

3 To display the **Borders** toolbar, move the mouse ⇗ over ⊞ and then press the left button.

Note: To hide the toolbar, repeat step **3** *.*

4 To display a list of the available line styles, move the mouse ⇗ over this area and then press the left button.

5 Move the mouse ⇗ over the line style you want to use and then press the left button.

Note: To view all the available line styles, use the scroll bar. For more information, refer to page 13.

- Create a Table
- Add a Row or Column
- Delete a Row or Column
- Delete a Table

- Change Column Width
- Merge Cells
- **Add Borders to a Table**
- Format a Table

Tip

When you print a table, the dotted lines separating the cells will not appear. To print lines around the cells, you must add borders.

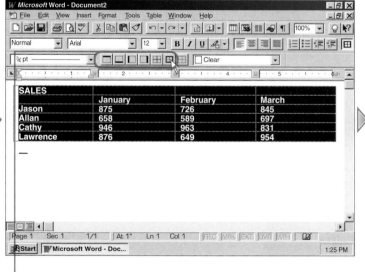

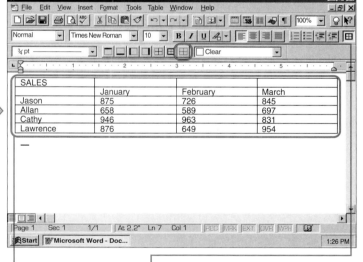

6 Move the mouse ⬡ over the border you want to add and then press the left button.

▦▦ ▣▣ Edges of cells

▦ Between cells

▣ Around cells

7 Repeat steps **4** to **6** for each border you want to add.

◆ The table displays the borders you selected.

Note: To deselect cells, move the mouse ⎁ outside the selected area and then press the left button.

REMOVE BORDERS

1 To select the cells you no longer want to display borders, perform steps **1** and **2** on page 170.

2 Move the mouse ⬡ over ▦ on the **Borders** toolbar and then press the left button.

FORMAT A TABLE

You can choose a design that best suits your table and then have Word apply the design for you.

SALES	January	February	March
Jason	875	726	845
Allan	658	589	697
Cathy	946	963	831
Lawrence	876	649	954

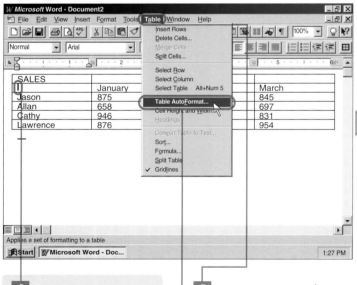

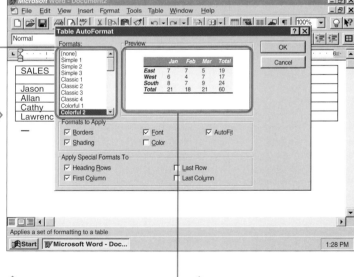

1 Move the mouse I anywhere over the table you want to change and then press the left button.

2 Move the mouse over **Table** and then press the left button.

3 Move the mouse over **Table AutoFormat** and then press the left button.

◆ The **Table AutoFormat** dialog box appears.

◆ This area displays a list of the available table designs.

◆ This area displays a sample of the highlighted table design.

4 Press ↓ or ↑ on your keyboard until a design you like appears (example: **Colorful 2**).

172

- Create a Table
- Add a Row or Column
- Delete a Row or Column
- Delete a Table

- Change Column Width
- Merge Cells
- Add Borders to a Table
- **Format a Table**

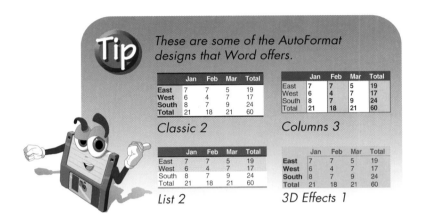

These are some of the AutoFormat designs that Word offers.

Classic 2

	Jan	Feb	Mar	Total
East	7	7	5	19
West	6	4	7	17
South	8	7	9	24
Total	21	18	21	60

Columns 3

	Jan	Feb	Mar	Total
East	7	7	5	19
West	6	4	7	17
South	8	7	9	24
Total	21	18	21	60

List 2

	Jan	Feb	Mar	Total
East	7	7	5	19
West	6	4	7	17
South	8	7	9	24
Total	21	18	21	60

3D Effects 1

	Jan	Feb	Mar	Total
East	7	7	5	19
West	6	4	7	17
South	8	7	9	24
Total	21	18	21	60

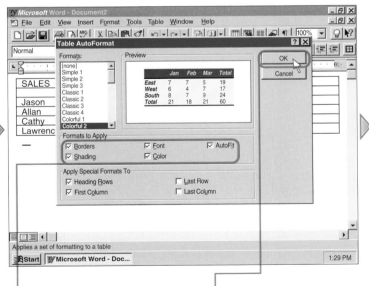

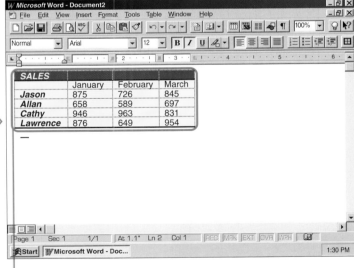

5 To apply or remove an option such as shading or color, move the mouse ⌖ over an option and then press the left button.

☑ The option will appear.

☐ The option will not appear.

6 To apply the design to your table, move the mouse ⌖ over **OK** and then press the left button.

◆ The table displays the design you selected.

REMOVE AUTOFORMAT

Perform steps **1** to **4**, selecting (**none**) in step **4**. Then press **Enter** on your keyboard.

173

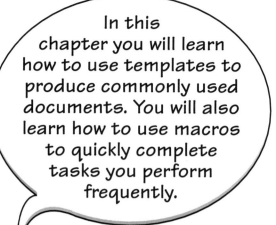

TIME SAVING FEATURES

- **Using a Template**
- **Record a Macro**
- **Run a Macro**

ON

5575 Copper Street
San Diego, CA 92100

ABC CORPORATION

MARKETING STRATEGY
FOR 1996

ABC CORPORATION'S BEST
OPPORTUNITY FOR EXPANSION

USING A TEMPLATE

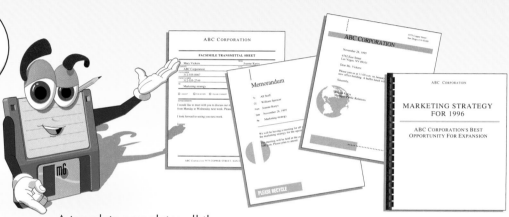

A template saves you time by providing the basic framework for a letter, fax, memo or report.

A template completes all the formatting so you can concentrate on the content of your document.

USING A TEMPLATE

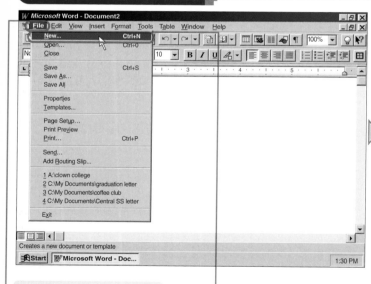 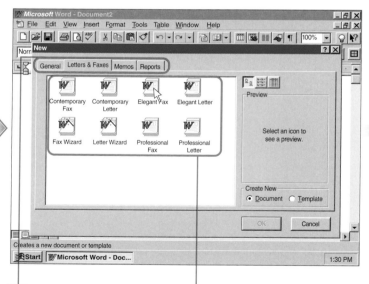

1 Move the mouse ⊥ over **File** and then press the left button.

2 Move the mouse ⊥ over **New** and then press the left button.

◆ The **New** dialog box appears.

3 Move the mouse ⊥ over the tab for the type of document you want to create (example: **Letters & Faxes**) and then press the left button.

4 Move the mouse ⊥ over the template you want to use (example: **Elegant Fax**) and then press the left button.

*Note: A template displaying **Wizard** in its name will help you prepare a document step by step.*

176

Tip

You can print and save a document you created with a template as you would print and save any document.

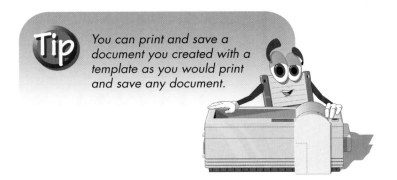

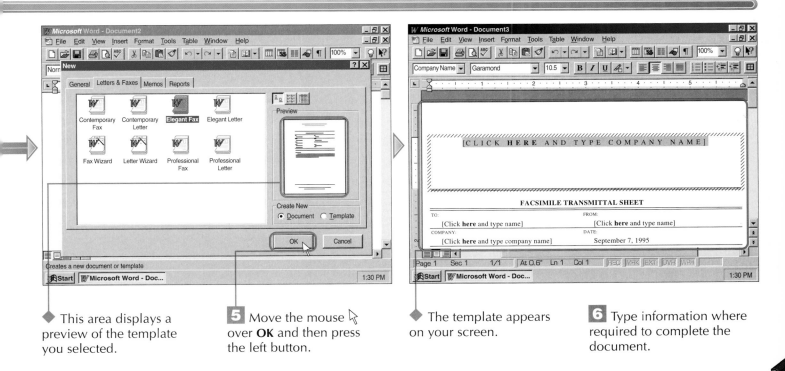

◆ This area displays a preview of the template you selected.

5 Move the mouse over **OK** and then press the left button.

◆ The template appears on your screen.

6 Type information where required to complete the document.

RECORD A MACRO

A macro saves you time by combining a series of commands into a single command.

RECORD A MACRO

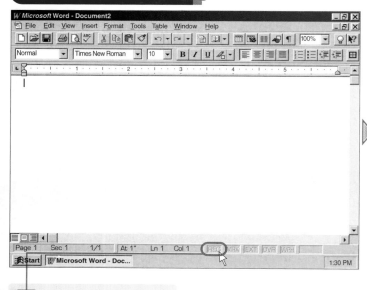

1 Move the mouse ⌖ over REC and then quickly press the left button twice.

◆ The **Record Macro** dialog box appears.

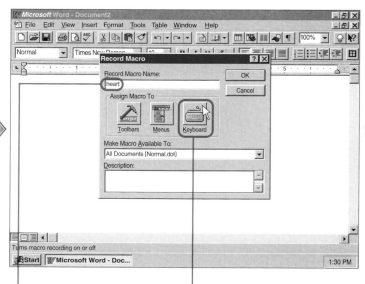

2 Type a name for the macro (example: **heart**).

Note: A macro name must begin with a letter and can only contain letters and numbers. The name cannot contain spaces.

3 To assign a keyboard shortcut to the macro, move the mouse ⌖ over **Keyboard** and then press the left button.

◆ The **Customize** dialog box appears.

- Using a Template
- **Record a Macro**
- Run a Macro

Tip

After you have recorded a macro, you can use the macro in any Word document.

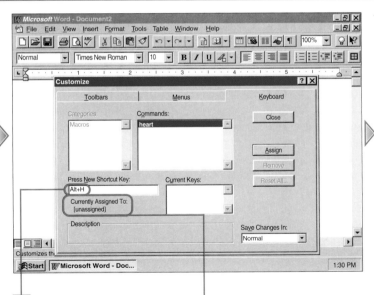

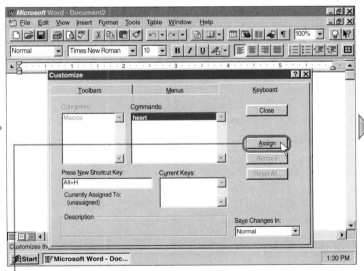

4 To enter the keyboard shortcut you want to assign to the macro, press and hold down **Alt** as you press a letter or number on your keyboard (example: **Alt** + **H**). Then release **Alt**.

◆ This area displays the word **[unassigned]**.

*Note: If the word **[unassigned]** is not displayed, the keyboard shortcut is already assigned to a macro. Press* **◆Backspace** *on your keyboard to delete the shortcut and then repeat step* **4**, *using a different letter or number.*

5 To assign the keyboard shortcut to the macro, move the mouse Ⓚ over **Assign** and then press the left button.

CONTINUED

Macros are ideal for tasks you perform over and over.

RECORD A MACRO (CONTINUED)

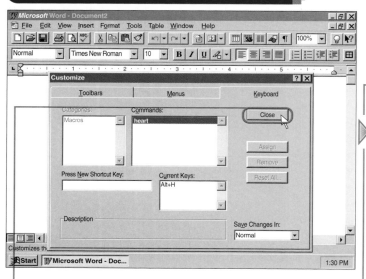

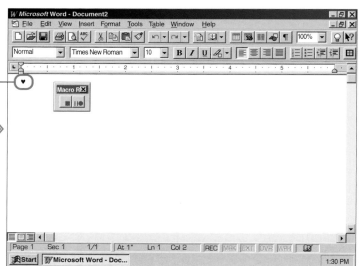

6 Move the mouse ⌖ over **Close** and then press the left button.

7 Perform the actions you want the macro to include.

◆ In this example, the ♥ symbol is inserted into the document. To insert a symbol, perform steps **2** to **8** starting on page 112.

Note: While recording a macro, you cannot use the mouse I to move the insertion point or select text.

• Using a Template
• **Record a Macro**
• **Run a Macro**

When you run a macro, Word automatically performs the series of commands you recorded.

RUN A MACRO

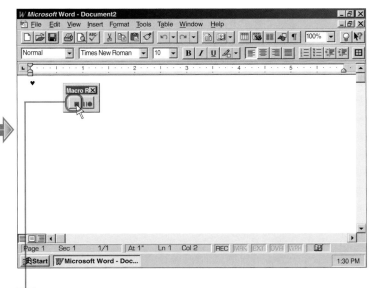

8 When you complete all the actions you want the macro to include, move the mouse ↖ over ■ and then press the left button.

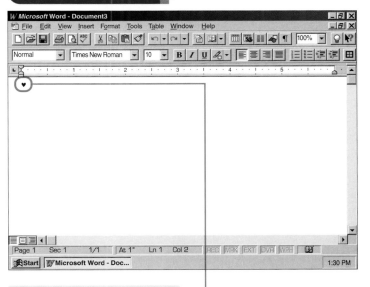

1 To run the macro, press the keyboard shortcut you assigned to the macro (example: Alt + H).

◆ In this example, the macro inserted the ♥ symbol into the document.

MERGE DOCUMENTS

Linda Wilson
999 Main Street
Burbank, CA 91505

John Smith
11 South Street
Los Angeles, CA 90013

You can use the Merge feature to produce personalized letters for each customer on a mailing list.

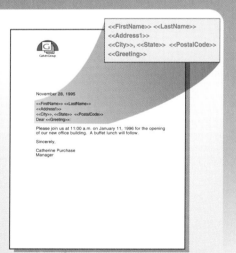

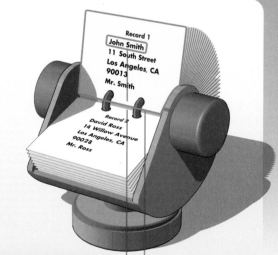

MAIN DOCUMENT

A main document contains the text that remains the same in each letter. It also contains codes that tell Word where to insert the personalized information that changes in each letter.

DATA SOURCE

A data source contains the information for each customer you want to receive the letter.

◆ The information for each customer is called a **record**.

◆ The information within each record is broken down into **fields**.

- • **Introduction**
- • Set Up a Main Document
- • Create a Data Source
- • Open a Data Source
- • Complete the Main Document
- • Merge Documents
- • Using Merge to Print Labels

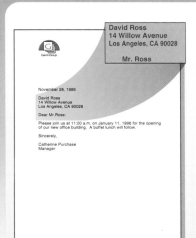

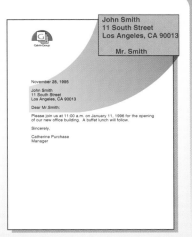

MERGED FILE

When you combine the main document and the data source, Word replaces the codes in the main document with the personalized information from the data source.

The main document contains the text that remains the same in each letter. It also contains codes that tell Word where to insert the personalized information that changes in each letter.

SET UP A MAIN DOCUMENT

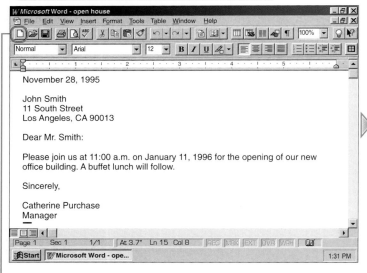

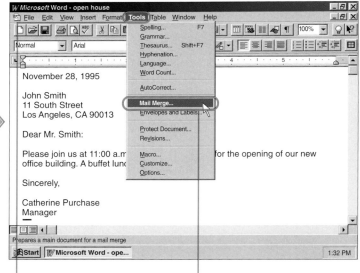

1 To create a new document, move the mouse ⌖ over 🗋 and then press the left button.

2 Create a letter for one of the customers on your mailing list (example: **John Smith**).

3 Save the document.

*Note: In this example, the document was named **open house**. For information on saving a document, refer to page 22.*

4 Move the mouse ⌖ over **Tools** and then press the left button.

5 Move the mouse ⌖ over **Mail Merge** and then press the left button.

- Introduction
- **Set Up a Main Document**
- Create a Data Source
- Open a Data Source
- Complete the Main Document
- Merge Documents
- Using Merge to Print Labels

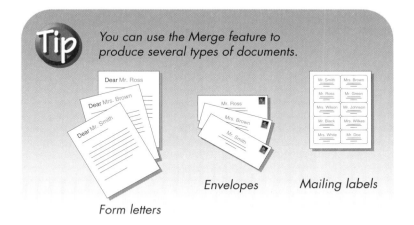

Tip

You can use the Merge feature to produce several types of documents.

Form letters

Envelopes

Mailing labels

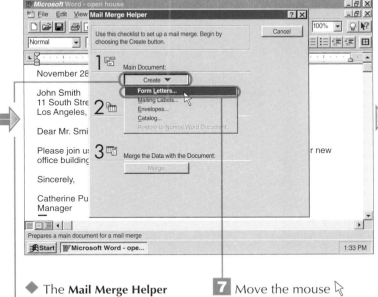

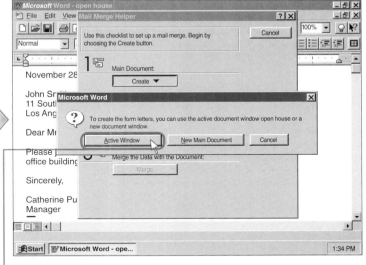

◆ The **Mail Merge Helper** dialog box appears.

6 To select the type of main document you want to create, move the mouse ⬚ over **Create** and then press the left button.

7 Move the mouse ⬚ over the type of document (example: **Form Letters**) and then press the left button.

◆ A dialog box appears.

8 To make the document displayed on your screen the main document, move the mouse ⬚ over **Active Window** and then press the left button.

Note: To continue, you must create or open a data source. To create a data source, refer to page 188. To open an existing data source, refer to page 194.

CREATE A DATA SOURCE

The data source contains information such as the name and address of each customer on your mailing list.

You only need to create a data source once. To use a data source you previously created, refer to page 194.

CREATE A DATA SOURCE

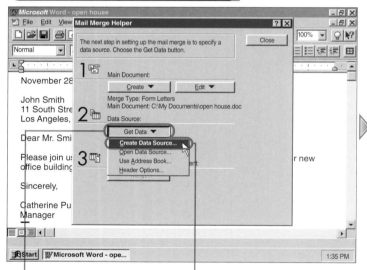

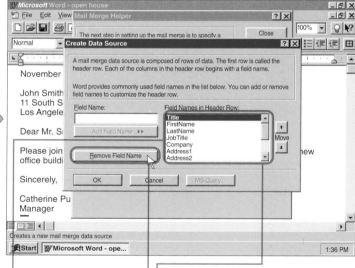

1 Move the mouse ⍓ over **Get Data** and then press the left button.

Note: You must set up a main document before creating a data source. To set up a main document, refer to page 186.

2 Move the mouse ⍓ over **Create Data Source** and then press the left button.

◆ The **Create Data Source** dialog box appears.

◆ Word provides a list of commonly used field names.

Note: To view all the available field names, use the scroll bar. For more information, refer to page 13.

REMOVE FIELD NAME

3 To remove a field name you will not use, move the mouse ⍓ over the field name and then press the left button.

4 Move the mouse ⍓ over **Remove Field Name** and then press the left button.

188

- Introduction
- Set Up a Main Document
- Create a Data Source
- Open a Data Source

- Complete the Main Document
- Merge Documents
- Using Merge to Print Labels

FIELD NAMES

A **field name** is a name given to a category of information in your data source, such as LastName or City.

November 28,1995

FirstName LastName
Address1
City, State PostalCode

Dear Greeting:

Please join us at 11:00 a.m. on January 11, 1996 for the opening of our new office building. A buffet lunch will follow.

Sincerely,

Catherine Purchase
Manager

November 28,1995

John Smith
11 South Street
Los Angeles, CA 90013

Dear Mr. Smith:

Please join us at 11:00 a.m. on January 11, 1996 for the opening of our new office building. A buffet lunch will follow.

Sincerely,

Catherine Purchase
Manager

Use your letter as a guide to help you decide which field names you need to include.

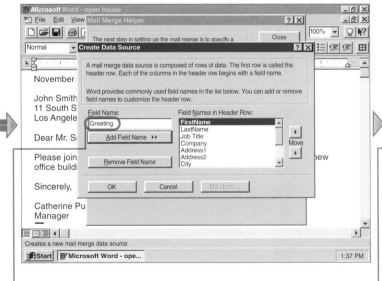

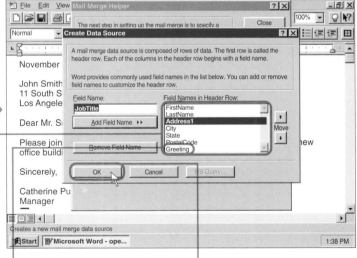

ADD FIELD NAME

5 To add a field name to the list, type the new field name and then press **Enter** on your keyboard.

Note: The field name cannot contain spaces and must begin with a letter.

◆ The field name appears in the list.

6 Remove or add field names until the list displays the field names you will use.

7 Move the mouse over **OK** and then press the left button.

CONTINUED

CREATE A
DATA SOURCE

After you save your data source, you can enter the information for each customer.

CREATE A DATA SOURCE (CONTINUED)

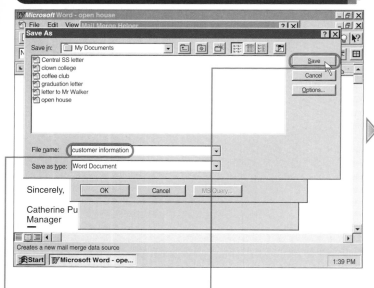

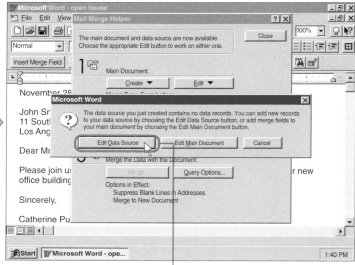

◆ The **Save As** dialog box appears so you can save the data source.

8 Type a name for the data source.

9 Move the mouse � over **Save** and then press the left button.

◆ A dialog box appears.

10 To enter the information for each customer on your mailing list, move the mouse � over **Edit Data Source** and then press the left button.

- Introduction
- Set Up a Main Document
- Create a Data Source
- Open a Data Source
- Complete the Main Document
- Merge Documents
- Using Merge to Print Labels

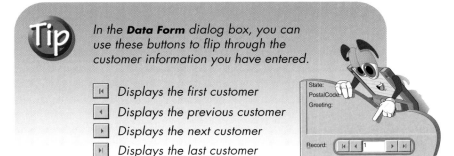

Tip

In the **Data Form** dialog box, you can use these buttons to flip through the customer information you have entered.

|◄ Displays the first customer

◄ Displays the previous customer

► Displays the next customer

►| Displays the last customer

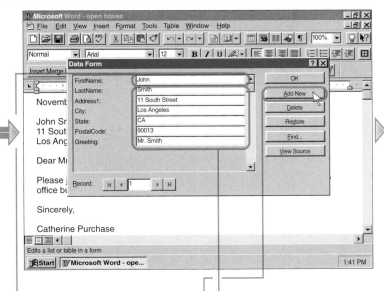

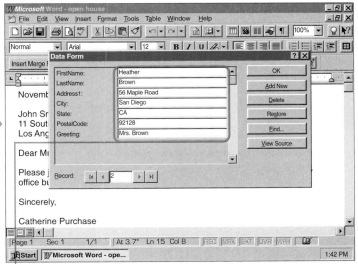

◆ The **Data Form** dialog box appears, displaying blank areas where you can enter the information for one customer.

11 Type the information that corresponds to the first blank area. To move to the next area, press **Tab** on your keyboard.

12 Repeat step **11** until you finish typing the information for the customer.

13 To add the information for the next customer on your mailing list, move the mouse � over **Add New** and then press the left button.

14 Repeat steps **11** to **13** for each customer on your mailing list.

CONTINUED

You can have Word display all the customer information you have entered in a table.

CREATE A DATA SOURCE (CONTINUED)

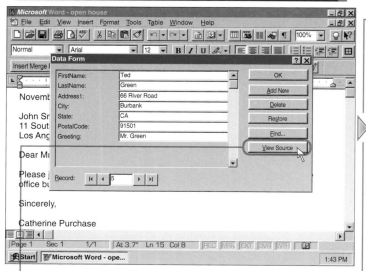

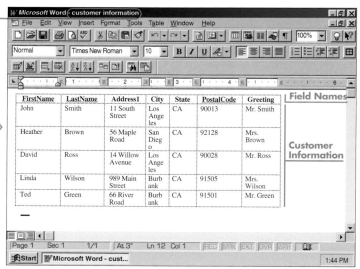

15 When you finish typing the information for all your customers, move the mouse ⤢ over **View Source** and then press the left button.

◆ The information you entered appears in a table.

◆ This area displays the name of the data source.

Note: If later on you want to update your customer information, you can open, edit, save and close the data source as you would any Word document.

- Introduction
- Set Up a Main Document
- **Create a Data Source**
- Open a Data Source
- Complete the Main Document
- Merge Documents
- Using Merge to Print Labels

Tip

Although some text does not fit on one line in the table, the text will print on one line when Word inserts it in the main document.

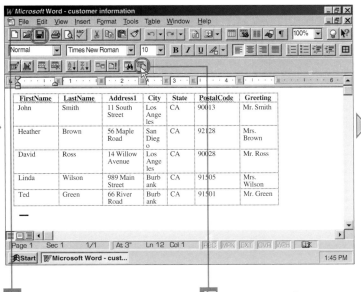

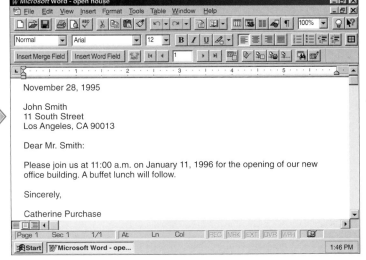

16 To save the information, move the mouse ⍾ over 🖫 and then press the left button.

17 To return to the main document, move the mouse ⍾ over 🖫 and then press the left button.

◆ The main document appears on your screen.

Note: To continue, you must complete the main document. To complete the main document, refer to page 196.

You only need to create a data source once. You can reuse the data source for all of your mailings.

OPEN A DATA SOURCE

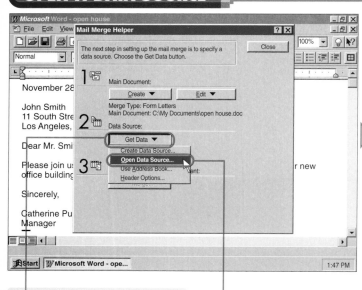

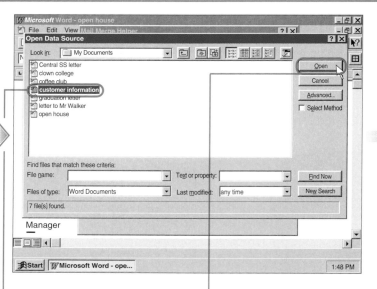

1 Move the mouse ⟩ over **Get Data** and then press the left button.

Note: You must set up a main document before opening a data source. To set up a main document, refer to page 186.

2 Move the mouse ⟩ over **Open Data Source** and then press the left button.

◆ The **Open Data Source** dialog box appears.

3 Move the mouse ⟩ over the name of the data source you want to open and then press the left button.

4 Move the mouse ⟩ over **Open** and then press the left button.

- Introduction
- Set Up a Main Document
- Create a Data Source
- **Open a Data Source**
- Complete the Main Document
- Merge Documents
- Using Merge to Print Labels

Tip

If you cannot find your data source in the **Open Data Source** dialog box, you can have Word search for the document.

Note: For more information, refer to page 30.

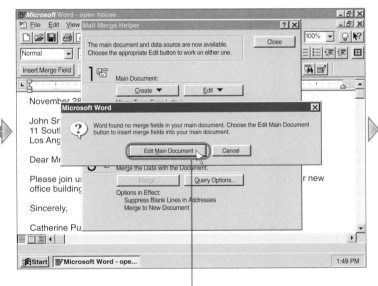

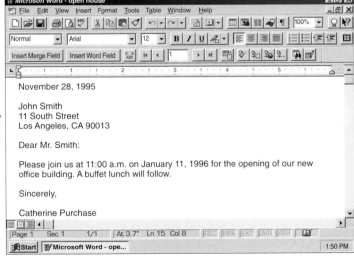

◆ A dialog box appears.

5 To return to the main document, move the mouse over **Edit Main Document** and then press the left button.

◆ The main document appears on your screen.

Note: To continue, you must complete the main document. To complete the main document, refer to page 196.

COMPLETE THE MAIN DOCUMENT

To complete the main document, you must tell Word what information you want to change in each letter.

COMPLETE THE MAIN DOCUMENT

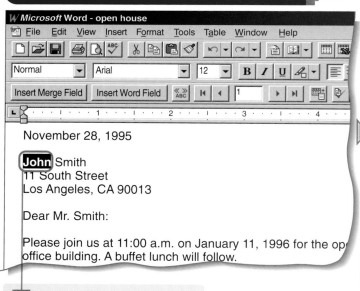

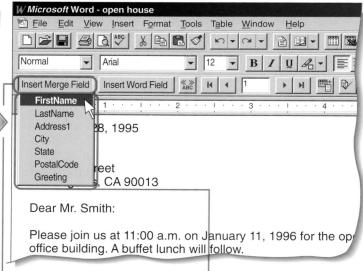

1 Select the first item of text you want to change in each letter. Do not select the spaces before or after the text. To select text, refer to page 10.

Note: You must first set up a main document. To set up a main document, refer to page 186.

2 To display a list of field names, move the mouse over **Insert Merge Field** and then press the left button.

3 Move the mouse over the field name for the information you want Word to insert and then press the left button.

- Introduction
- Set Up a Main Document
- Create a Data Source
- Open a Data Source
- **Complete the Main Document**
- Merge Documents
- Using Merge to Print Labels

Tip

When you merge the main document and the data source, the field names are replaced by the customer information.

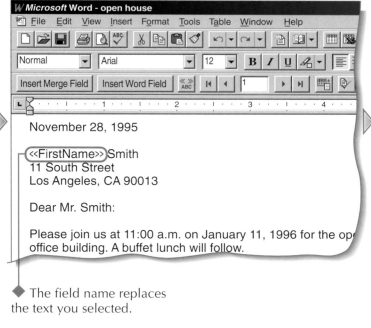

November 28, 1995

<<FirstName>> Smith
11 South Street
Los Angeles, CA 90013

Dear Mr. Smith:

Please join us at 11:00 a.m. on January 11, 1996 for the op
office building. A buffet lunch will follow.

◆ The field name replaces the text you selected.

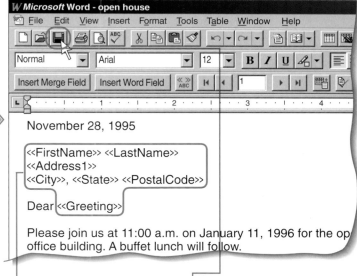

November 28, 1995

<<FirstName>> <<LastName>>
<<Address1>>
<<City>>, <<State>> <<PostalCode>>

Dear <<Greeting>>

Please join us at 11:00 a.m. on January 11, 1996 for the op
office building. A buffet lunch will follow.

4 Repeat steps **1** to **3** for all the text you want Word to change in each letter.

5 To save the document, move the mouse over and then press the left button.

Note: To continue, you must merge the main document and the data source. To merge the documents, refer to page 198.

197

MERGE DOCUMENTS

You can combine the main document and the data source to create a personalized letter for each customer on your mailing list.

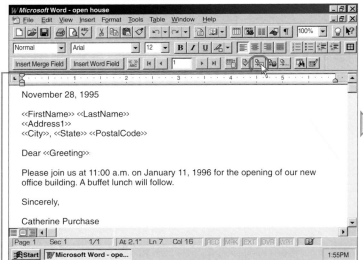

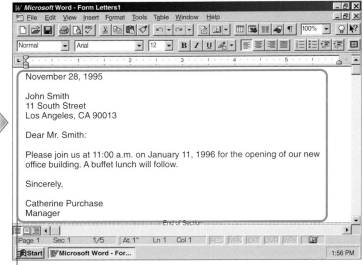

1 To merge the main document and the data source, move the mouse ⌖ over 🔲 and then press the left button.

◆ Word creates a personalized letter for each customer.

2 To view the letters, press **PageDown** on your keyboard several times.

◆ You can edit the letters as you would edit any document.

- Introduction
- Set Up a Main Document
- Create a Data Source
- Open a Data Source
- Complete the Main Document
- **Merge Documents**
- Using Merge to Print Labels

Tip

To conserve hard disk space, do not save the merged document.

*To quickly recreate the document, open the main document (example: **open house**). Then perform step* **1** *on page 198.*

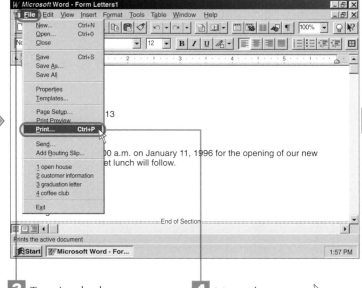

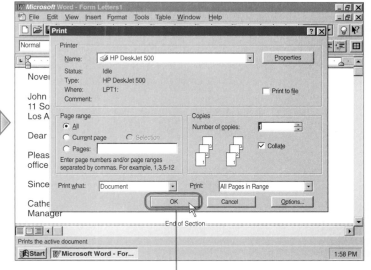

3 To print the letters, move the mouse ⟨ over **File** and then press the left button.

4 Move the mouse ⟨ over **Print** and then press the left button.

◆ The **Print** dialog box appears.

5 Move the mouse ⟨ over **OK** and then press the left button.

You can use the Merge feature to create a mailing label for every customer on your mailing list.

USING MERGE TO PRINT LABELS

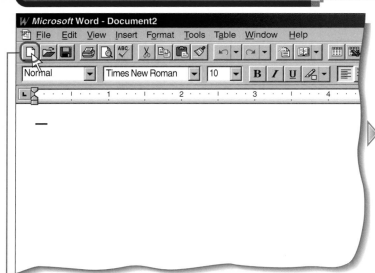

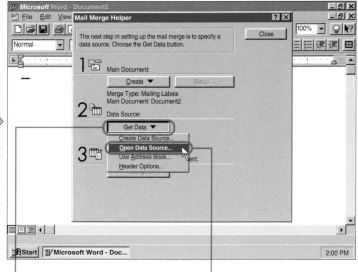

1 To create a new document, move the mouse ⌖ over ☐ and then press the left button.

2 To tell Word that you want to create mailing labels, perform steps **4** to **8** starting on page 186, selecting **Mailing Labels** in step **7**.

3 To open a data source you previously created, move the mouse ⌖ over **Get Data** and then press the left button.

*Note: For information on data sources, refer to the **Tip** on page 201.*

4 Move the mouse ⌖ over **Open Data Source** and then press the left button.

- Introduction
- Set Up a Main Document
- Create a Data Source
- Open a Data Source

- Complete the Main Document
- Merge Documents
- **Using Merge to Print Labels**

Tip

A **data source** is a document that contains information about each customer on your mailing list.

Note: To create a data source, refer to page 188.

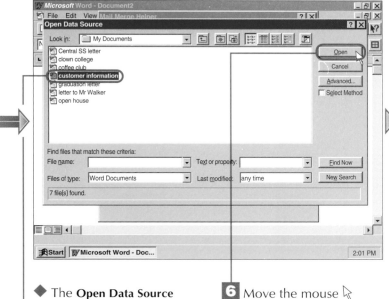

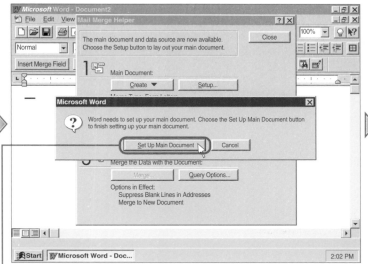

◆ The **Open Data Source** dialog box appears.

5 Move the mouse over the name of the data source you want to use and then press the left button.

6 Move the mouse over **Open** and then press the left button.

◆ A dialog box appears.

7 To set up the labels, move the mouse over **Set Up Main Document** and then press the left button.

CONTINUED

USING MERGE TO PRINT LABELS

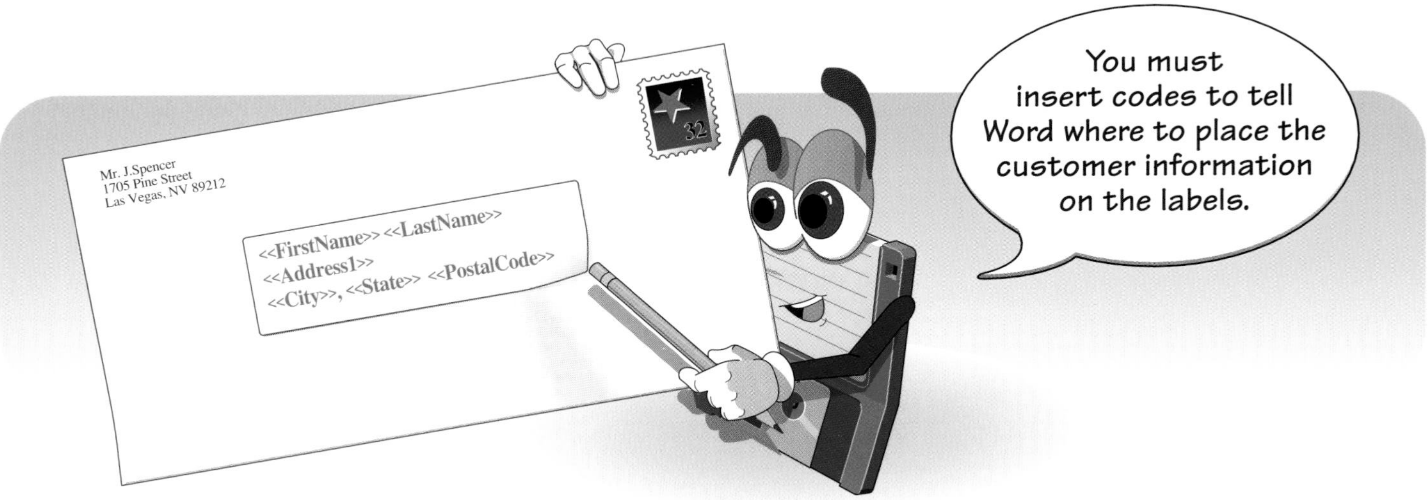

USING MERGE TO PRINT LABELS (CONTINUED)

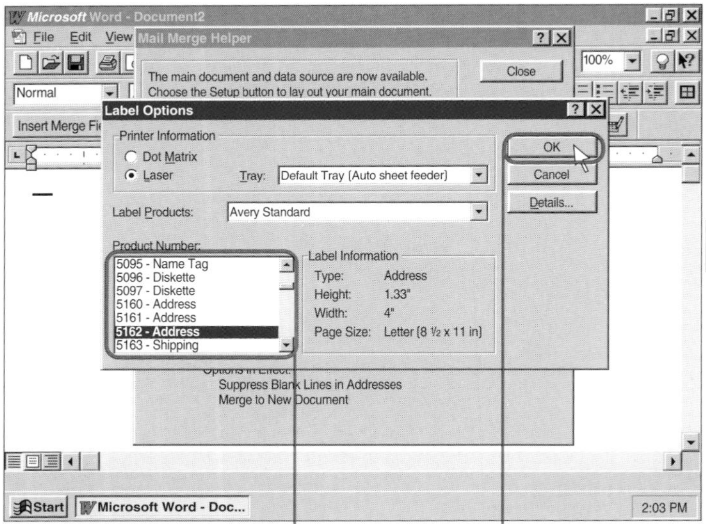

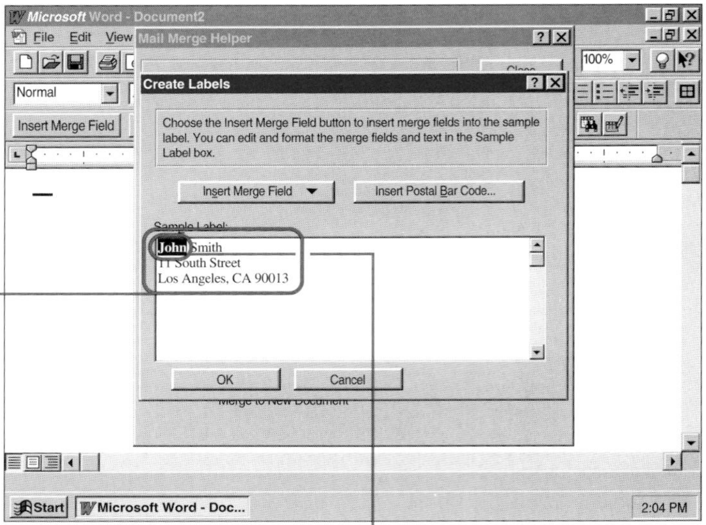

◆ The **Label Options** dialog box appears.

8 Move the mouse over the type of label you want to use and then press the left button. Refer to the label packaging for help in selecting the correct type.

9 Move the mouse over **OK** and then press the left button.

◆ The **Create Labels** dialog box appears.

10 Type a label for one of the customers on your mailing list.

11 Select the first item of text you want to change in each label. Do not select the spaces before or after the text.

Note: To select text, refer to page 10.

- Introduction
- Set Up a Main Document
- Create a Data Source
- Open a Data Source
- Complete the Main Document
- Merge Documents
- **Using Merge to Print Labels**

If you want to print a label for only one customer, use the Label feature.

Note: For information on printing a label, refer to page 76.

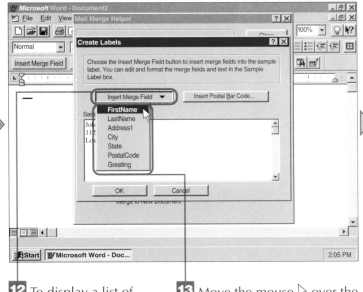

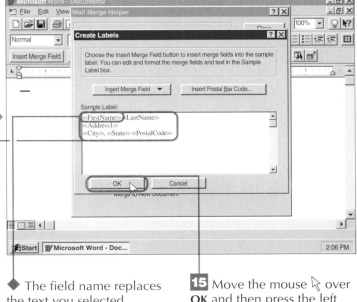

12 To display a list of field names, move the mouse ⌖ over **Insert Merge Field** and then press the left button.

13 Move the mouse ⌖ over the field name for the information you want Word to insert and then press the left button.

Note: The field names that appear depend on the field names you specified when you created the data source.

◆ The field name replaces the text you selected.

14 Repeat steps **11** to **13** for all the text you want Word to change in each label.

15 Move the mouse ⌖ over **OK** and then press the left button.

CONTINUED

203

USING MERGE TO PRINT LABELS

After you merge the labels and the data source, you can print the labels.

USING MERGE TO PRINT LABELS (CONTINUED)

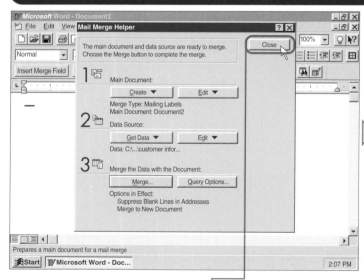

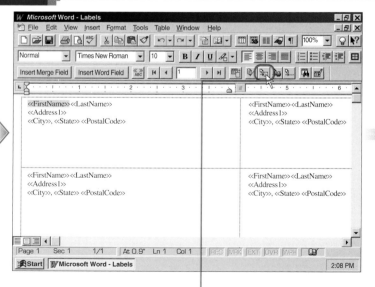

◆ The **Mail Merge Helper** dialog box reappears.

16 Move the mouse ⬚ over **Close** and then press the left button.

17 Save the labels as you would save any document.

*Note: In this example, the document was named **Labels**. For information on saving a document, refer to page 22.*

18 To merge the labels and the data source, move the mouse ⬚ over 🔲 and then press the left button.

204

- Introduction
- Set Up a Main Document
- Create a Data Source
- Open a Data Source

- Complete the Main Document
- Merge Documents
- **Using Merge to Print Labels**

Tip

To conserve hard disk space, do not save the merged labels.

To quickly recreate the labels, open the label document you saved in step **17** on page 204. Then perform step **18**.

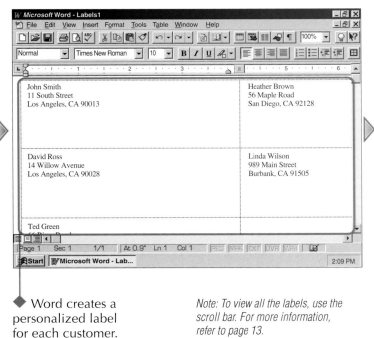

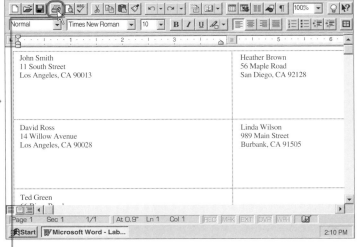

◆ Word creates a personalized label for each customer.

Note: To view all the labels, use the scroll bar. For more information, refer to page 13.

19 To print all the labels, move the mouse ⬚ over 🖨 and then press the left button.

205

INDEX

INDEX

INDEX

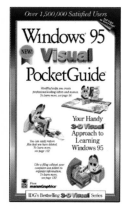

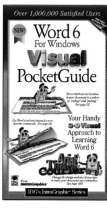

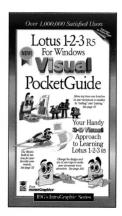

Over 2,000,000 Satisfied Users!

from:
maranGraphics™

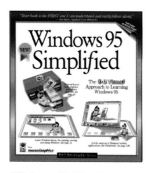

Windows 95 Simplified
ISBN 1-56884-662-2
$19.99 USA/£18.99 UK

Windows 3.1 Simplified
ISBN 1-56884-654-1
$19.99 USA/£18.99 UK

Computers Simplified 2nd Edition
ISBN 1-56884-676-2
$19.99 USA/£18.99 UK

Word 6 For Windows Simplified
ISBN 1-56884-660-6
$19.99 USA/£18.99 UK

Excel 5 For Windows Simplified
ISBN 1-56884-664-9
$19.99 USA/£18.99 UK

3-D Visual Dictionary of Computing
ISBN 1-56884-678-9
$19.99 USA/£18.99 UK

WordPerfect 6.1 For Windows Simplified
ISBN 1-56884-665-7
$19.99 USA/£18.99 UK

Lotus 1-2-3 R5 For Windows Simplified
ISBN 1-56884-670-3
$19.99 USA/£18.99 UK

Microsoft Office 4.2 For Windows Simplified
ISBN 1-56884-673-8
$27.99 USA/£26.99 UK

Coming Soon!

Internet Simplified
ISBN 1-56884-658-4
$19.99 USA/£18.99 UK

Excel for Windows 95 Simplified
ISBN 1-56884-682-7
$19.99 USA/£18.99 UK

Visit our Web site at:
http://www.maran.com

FOR 3-D VISUAL CORPORATE ORDERS, PLEASE CALL : 800 . 469 . 6616 ext. 206

The fun & easy way to learn about computers and more!

Windows 3.1 For Dummies,™ 2nd Edition
by Andy Rathbone

ISBN: 1-56884-182-5
$16.95 USA/$22.95 Canada

MORE Windows For Dummies™
by Andy Rathbone

ISBN: 1-56884-048-9
$19.95 USA/$26.95 Canada

DOS For Dummies,® 2nd Edition
by Dan Gookin

ISBN: 1-878058-75-4
$16.95 USA/$22.95 Canada

The Internet For Dummies™
by John Levine & Carol Baroudi

ISBN: 1-56884-024-1
$19.95 USA/$26.95 Canada

Personal Finance For Dummies™
by Eric Tyson

ISBN: 1-56884-150-7
$16.95 USA/$22.95 Canada

PCs For Dummies,™ 2nd Edition
by Dan Gookin & Andy Rathbone

ISBN: 1-56884-078-0
$16.95 USA/$22.95 Canada

Macs For Dummies,™ 2nd Edition
by David Pogue

ISBN: 1-56884-051-9
$19.95 USA/$26.95 Canada

Over 12 Million in print!

Here's a complete listing of IDG's...*For Dummies* Titles

Title	Author	ISBN #	Price
DATABASE			
Access 2 For Dummies™	by Scott Palmer	ISBN: 1-56884-090-X	$19.95 USA/$26.95 Canada
Access Programming For Dummies™	by Rob Krumm	ISBN: 1-56884-091-8	$19.95 USA/$26.95 Canada
Approach 3 For Windows For Dummies™	by Doug Lowe	ISBN: 1-56884-233-3	$19.99 USA/$26.99 Canada
dBASE For DOS For Dummies™	by Scott Palmer & Michael Stabler	ISBN: 1-56884-188-4	$19.95 USA/$26.95 Canada
dBASE For Windows For Dummies™	by Scott Palmer	ISBN: 1-56884-179-5	$19.95 USA/$26.95 Canada
dBASE 5 For Windows Programming For Dummies™	by Ted Coombs & Jason Coombs	ISBN: 1-56884-215-5	$19.99 USA/$26.99 Canada
FoxPro 2.6 For Windows For Dummies™	by John Kaufeld	ISBN: 1-56884-187-6	$19.95 USA/$26.95 Canada
Paradox 5 For Windows For Dummies™	by John Kaufeld	ISBN: 1-56884-185-X	$19.95 USA/$26.95 Canada
DESKTOP PUBLISHING/ILLUSTRATION/GRAPHICS			
CorelDRAW! 5 For Dummies™	by Deke McClelland	ISBN: 1-56884-157-4	$19.95 USA/$26.95 Canada
CorelDRAW! For Dummies™	by Deke McClelland	ISBN: 1-56884-042-X	$19.95 USA/$26.95 Canada
Harvard Graphics 2 For Windows For Dummies™	by Roger C. Parker	ISBN: 1-56884-092-6	$19.95 USA/$26.95 Canada
PageMaker 5 For Macs For Dummies™	by Galen Gruman & Deke McClelland	ISBN: 1-56884-178-7	$19.95 USA/$26.95 Canada
PageMaker 5 For Windows For Dummies™	by Deke McClelland & Galen Gruman	ISBN: 1-56884-160-4	$19.95 USA/$26.95 Canada
QuarkXPress 3.3 For Dummies™	by Galen Gruman & Barbara Assadi	ISBN: 1-56884-217-1	$19.99 USA/$26.99 Canada
FINANCE/PERSONAL FINANCE/TEST TAKING REFERENCE			
QuickBooks "X" For Dummies™	by Stephen L. Nelson	ISBN: 1-56884-227-9	$19.99 USA/$26.99 Canada
Quicken "X" For DOS For Dummies™, 2nd Edition	by Stephen L. Nelson	ISBN: 1-56884-210-4	$19.95 USA/$26.95 Canada
Quicken "X" For Macs For Dummies™	by Stephen L. Nelson	ISBN: 1-56884-211-2	$19.95 USA/$26.95 Canada
Quicken "X" For Windows For Dummies™, 2nd Edition	by Stephen L. Nelson	ISBN: 1-56884-209-0	$19.95 USA/$26.95 Canada
The SAT I For Dummies™	by Suzee Vlk	ISBN: 1-56884-213-9	$14.99 USA/$20.99 Canada
TurboTax For Windows For Dummies™	by Gail A. Perry, CPA	ISBN: 1-56884-228-7	$19.99 USA/$26.99 Canada
GROUPWARE/INTEGRATED			
Lotus Notes 3.0/3.1 For Dummies™	by Paul Freeland & Stephen Londergan	ISBN: 1-56884-212-0	$19.95 USA/$26.95 Canada
Microsoft Office 4 For Windows For Dummies™	by Roger C. Parker	ISBN: 1-56884-183-3	$19.95 USA/$26.95 Canada
Microsoft Works For Windows 3 For Dummies™	by David C. Kay	ISBN: 1-56884-214-7	$19.99 USA/$26.99 Canada

FOR MORE INFO OR TO ORDER, PLEASE CALL ▶ 800.762.2974 For volume discounts & special orders please call Tony Real, Special Sales, at 415.312.0644

Title	Author	ISBN #	Price
INTERNET/COMMUNICATIONS/NETWORKING			
CompuServe For Dummies™	by Wallace Wang	ISBN: 1-56884-181-7	$19.95 USA/$26.95 Canada
Modems For Dummies™, 2nd Edition	by Tina Rathbone	ISBN: 1-56884-223-6	$19.99 USA/$26.99 Canada
Modems For Dummies™	by Tina Rathbone	ISBN: 1-56884-001-2	$19.95 USA/$26.95 Canada
MORE Internet For Dummies™	by John Levine & Margaret Levine Young	ISBN: 1-56884-164-7	$19.95 USA/$26.95 Canada
NetWare For Dummies™	by Ed Tittel & Deni Connor	ISBN: 1-56884-003-9	$19.95 USA/$26.95 Canada
Networking For Dummies™	by Doug Lowe	ISBN: 1-56884-079-9	$19.95 USA/$26.95 Canada
ProComm Plus 2 For Windows For Dummies™	by Wallace Wang	ISBN: 1-56884-219-8	$19.99 USA/$26.99 Canada
The Internet Help Desk For Dummies™	by John Kaufeld	ISBN: 1-56884-238-4	$16.99 USA/$22.99 Canada
The3 Internet For Dummies™, 2nd Edition	by John Levine & Carol Baroudi	ISBN: 1-56884-222-8	$19.99 USA/$26.99 Canada
The Internet For Macs For Dummies™	by Charles Seiter	ISBN: 1-56884-184-1	$19.95 USA/$26.95 Canada
MACINTOSH			
Mac Programming For Dummies™	by Dan Parks Sydow	ISBN: 1-56884-173-6	$19.95 USA/$26.95 Canada
Macintosh System 7.5 For Dummies™	by Bob LeVitus	ISBN: 1-56884-197-3	$19.95 USA/$26.95 Canada
MORE Macs For Dummies™	by David Pogue	ISBN: 1-56884-087-X	$19.95 USA/$26.95 Canada
PageMaker 5 For Macs For Dummies™	by Galen Gruman & Deke McClelland	ISBN: 1-56884-178-7	$19.95 USA/$26.95 Canada
QuarkXPress 3.3 For Dummies™	by Galen Gruman & Barbara Assadi	ISBN: 1-56884-217-1	$19.99 USA/$26.99 Canada
Upgrading and Fixing Macs For Dummies™	by Kearney Rietmann & Frank Higgins	ISBN: 1-56884-189-2	$19.95 USA/$26.95 Canada
MULTIMEDIA			
Multimedia & CD-ROMs For Dummies™, Interactive Multimedia Value Pack	by Andy Rathbone	ISBN: 1-56884-225-2	$29.95 USA/$39.95 Canada
Multimedia & CD-ROMs For Dummies™	by Andy Rathbone	ISBN: 1-56884-089-6	$19.95 USA/$26.95 Canada
OPERATING SYSTEMS/DOS			
MORE DOS For Dummies™	by Dan Gookin	ISBN: 1-56884-046-2	$19.95 USA/$26.95 Canada
S.O.S. For DOS™	by Katherine Murray	ISBN: 1-56884-043-8	$12.95 USA/$16.95 Canada
OS/2 For Dummies™	by Andy Rathbone	ISBN: 1-878058-76-2	$19.95 USA/$26.95 Canada
UNIX			
UNIX For Dummies™	by John Levine & Margaret Levine Young	ISBN: 1-878058-58-4	$19.95 USA/$26.95 Canada
WINDOWS			
S.O.S. For Windows™	by Katherine Murray	ISBN: 1-56884-045-4	$12.95 USA/$16.95 Canada
Windows "X" For Dummies™, 3rd Edition	by Andy Rathbone	ISBN: 1-56884-240-6	$19.99 USA/$26.99 Canada
PCS/HARDWARE			
Illustrated Computer Dictionary For Dummies™	by Dan Gookin, Wally Wang, & Chris Van Buren	ISBN: 1-56884-004-7	$12.95 USA/$16.95 Canada
Upgrading and Fixing PCs For Dummies™	by Andy Rathbone	ISBN: 1-56884-002-0	$19.95 USA/$26.95 Canada
PRESENTATION/AUTOCAD			
AutoCAD For Dummies™	by Bud Smith	ISBN: 1-56884-191-4	$19.95 USA/$26.95 Canada
PowerPoint 4 For Windows For Dummies™	by Doug Lowe	ISBN: 1-56884-161-2	$16.95 USA/$22.95 Canada
PROGRAMMING			
Borland C++ For Dummies™	by Michael Hyman	ISBN: 1-56884-162-0	$19.95 USA/$26.95 Canada
"Borland's New Language Product" For Dummies™	by Neil Rubenking	ISBN: 1-56884-200-7	$19.95 USA/$26.95 Canada
C For Dummies™	by Dan Gookin	ISBN: 1-878058-78-9	$19.95 USA/$26.95 Canada
C++ For Dummies™	by S. Randy Davis	ISBN: 1-56884-163-9	$19.95 USA/$26.95 Canada
Mac Programming For Dummies™	by Dan Parks Sydow	ISBN: 1-56884-173-6	$19.95 USA/$26.95 Canada
QBasic Programming For Dummies™	by Douglas Hergert	ISBN: 1-56884-093-4	$19.95 USA/$26.95 Canada
Visual Basic "X" For Dummies™, 2nd Edition	by Wallace Wang	ISBN: 1-56884-230-9	$19.99 USA/$26.99 Canada
Visual Basic 3 For Dummies™	by Wallace Wang	ISBN: 1-56884-076-4	$19.95 USA/$26.95 Canada
SPREADSHEET			
1-2-3 For Dummies™	by Greg Harvey	ISBN: 1-878058-60-6	$16.95 USA/$22.95 Canada
1-2-3 For Windows 5 For Dummies™, 2nd Edition	by John Walkenbach	ISBN: 1-56884-216-3	$16.95 USA/$22.95 Canada
1-2-3 For Windows For Dummies™	by John Walkenbach	ISBN: 1-56884-052-7	$16.95 USA/$22.95 Canada
Excel 5 For Macs For Dummies™	by Greg Harvey	ISBN: 1-56884-186-8	$19.95 USA/$26.95 Canada
Excel For Dummies™, 2nd Edition	by Greg Harvey	ISBN: 1-56884-050-0	$16.95 USA/$22.95 Canada
MORE Excel 5 For Windows For Dummies™	by Greg Harvey	ISBN: 1-56884-207-4	$19.95 USA/$26.95 Canada
Quattro Pro 6 For Windows For Dummies™	by John Walkenbach	ISBN: 1-56884-174-4	$19.95 USA/$26.95 Canada
Quattro Pro For DOS For Dummies™	by John Walkenbach	ISBN: 1-56884-023-3	$16.95 USA/$22.95 Canada
UTILITIES			
Norton Utilities 8 For Dummies™	by Beth Slick	ISBN: 1-56884-166-3	$19.95 USA/$26.95 Canada
VCRS/CAMCORDERS			
VCRs & Camcorders For Dummies™	by Andy Rathbone & Gordon McComb	ISBN: 1-56884-229-5	$14.99 USA/$20.99 Canada
WORD PROCESSING			
Ami Pro For Dummies™	by Jim Meade	ISBN: 1-56884-049-7	$19.95 USA/$26.95 Canada
More Word For Windows 6 For Dummies™	by Doug Lowe	ISBN: 1-56884-165-5	$19.95 USA/$26.95 Canada
MORE WordPerfect 6 For Windows For Dummies™	by Margaret Levine Young & David C. Kay	ISBN: 1-56884-206-6	$19.95 USA/$26.95 Canada
MORE WordPerfect 6 For DOS For Dummies™	by Wallace Wang, edited by Dan Gookin	ISBN: 1-56884-047-0	$19.95 USA/$26.95 Canada
S.O.S. For WordPerfect™	by Katherine Murray	ISBN: 1-56884-053-5	$12.95 USA/$16.95 Canada
Word 6 For Macs For Dummies™	by Dan Gookin	ISBN: 1-56884-190-6	$19.95 USA/$26.95 Canada
Word For Windows 6 For Dummies™	by Dan Gookin	ISBN: 1-56884-075-6	$16.95 USA/$22.95 Canada
Word For Windows 2 For Dummies™	by Dan Gookin	ISBN: 1-878058-86-X	$16.95 USA/$22.95 Canada
WordPerfect 6 For Dummies™	by Dan Gookin	ISBN: 1-878058-77-0	$16.95 USA/$22.95 Canada
WordPerfect For Dummies™	by Dan Gookin	ISBN: 1-878058-52-5	$16.95 USA/$22.95 Canada
WordPerfect For Windows For Dummies™	by Margaret Levine Young & David C. Kay	ISBN: 1-56884-032-2	$16.95 USA/$22.95 Canada

TRADE & INDIVIDUAL ORDERS

Phone: **(800) 762-2974** *or* **(317) 895-5200**
(8 a.m.–6 p.m., CST, weekdays)
FAX : **(317) 895-5298**

CORPORATE ORDERS FOR 3-D VISUAL™ SERIES

Phone: **(800) 469-6616** *ext.* **206**
(8 a.m.–5 p.m., EST, weekdays)
FAX : **(905) 890-9434**

Qty	ISBN	Title	Price	Total

Shipping & Handling Charges

	Description	First book	Each add'l. book	Total
Domestic	Normal	$4.50	$1.50	$
	Two Day Air	$8.50	$2.50	$
	Overnight	$18.00	$3.00	$
International	Surface	$8.00	$8.00	$
	Airmail	$16.00	$16.00	$
	DHL Air	$17.00	$17.00	$

Subtotal _____

CA residents add
applicable sales tax _____

IN, MA and MD
residents add
5% sales tax _____

IL residents add
6.25% sales tax _____

RI residents add
7% sales tax _____

TX residents add
8.25% sales tax _____

Shipping _____

Total _____

Ship to:

Name_____

Address_____

Company _____

City/State/Zip _____

Daytime Phone_____

Payment: ☐ Check to IDG Books (US Funds Only)

☐ Visa   ☐ Mastercard   ☐ American Express

Card # _____ Exp. _____ Signature_____

IDG Books Education Group
Jim Kelly, Director of Education Sales – 9 Village Circle, Ste. 450, Westlake, TX 76262
800-434-2086 Phone • 817-430-5852 Fax • 8:30-5:00 CST

IDG BOOKS WORLDWIDE REGISTRATION CARD

RETURN THIS REGISTRATION CARD FOR FREE CATALOG

Title of this book: Word For Windows 95 Simplified

My overall rating of this book: ❑ Very good [1]   ❑ Good [2]   ❑ Satisfactory [3]   ❑ Fair [4]   ❑ Poor [5]

How I first heard about this book:

❑ Found in bookstore; name: [6] _____   ❑ Book review: [7] _____

❑ Advertisement: [8] _____   ❑ Catalog: [9] _____

❑ Word of mouth; heard about book from friend, co-worker, etc.: [10] _____   ❑ Other: [11] _____

What I liked most about this book:

_____

_____

_____

What I would change, add, delete, etc., in future editions of this book:

_____

_____

_____

Other comments:

_____

_____

Number of computer books I purchase in a year: ❑ 1 [12]   ❑ 2-5 [13]   ❑ 6-10 [14]   ❑ More than 10 [15]

I would characterize my computer skills as: ❑ Beginner [16] ❑ Intermediate [17] ❑ Advanced [18] ❑ Professional [19]

I use ❑ DOS [20]   ❑ Windows [21]   ❑ OS/2 [22]   ❑ Unix [23]   ❑ Macintosh [24]   ❑ Other: [25] _____
(please specify)

I would be interested in new books on the following subjects:
(please check all that apply, and use the spaces provided to identify specific software)

❑ Word processing: [26] _____   ❑ Spreadsheets: [27] _____

❑ Data bases: [28] _____   ❑ Desktop publishing: [29] _____

❑ File Utilities: [30] _____   ❑ Money management: [31] _____

❑ Networking: [32] _____   ❑ Programming languages: [33] _____

❑ Other: [34] _____

I use a PC at (please check all that apply): ❑ home [35]   ❑ work [36]   ❑ school [37]   ❑ other: [38] _____

The disks I prefer to use are ❑ 5.25 [39]   ❑ 3.5 [40]   ❑ other: [41] _____

I have a CD ROM: ❑ yes [42]   ❑ no [43]

I plan to buy or upgrade computer hardware this year: ❑ yes [44]   ❑ no [45]

I plan to buy or upgrade computer software this year: ❑ yes [46]   ❑ no [47]

Name: _____   Business title: [48] _____   Type of Business: [49] _____

Address (❑ home [50] ❑ work [51] /Company name: _____)

Street/Suite# _____

City [52] /State [53] /Zipcode [54]: _____   Country [55] _____

❑ **I liked this book!** You may quote me by name in future
IDG Books Worldwide promotional materials.

My daytime phone number is _____

IDG BOOKS
THE WORLD OF COMPUTER KNOWLEDGE

❏ YES!

Please keep me informed about IDG's World of Computer Knowledge.
Send me the latest IDG Books catalog.